FEARLESS FEMALE LEADERSHIP

9 ESSENTIAL STRATEGIES TO OVERCOME GENDER BIASES, BUILD CONFIDENCE, AND EMPOWER YOUR CAREER

MARGUERITE ALLOLDING

SHE LEADS STRATEGIES, LLC

1st Editon

Author: Marguerite Allolding

Publisher: She Leads Strategies, LLC

TABLE OF CONTENTS

INTRODUCTION

Did you know that as of 2020, women held a global average of 19.7% of board seats in several organizations? Although this is a significant figure compared to the 2.8% since 2018, it still underscores the underrepresentation of women in top decision-making roles (Tina, 2023).

Imagine you're in a meeting where you've got these brilliant ideas to share, and of course, you do. However, they get flipped over, only to be praised moments later when a male colleague presents the same concept. Or picture the frustration of constantly needing to prove yourself, working twice as hard to gain the same recognition and respect as your male counterparts who might have done only 30% of the amount of work you got done. These all-too-familiar scenarios highlight the challenges women face in the world of female leadership.

But here's another eye-opener: the leadership training market is projected to reach a staggering $26.7 billion by 2024 (Technavio, 2020). Undoubtedly, the demand for effective leadership is soaring, and the 2023 Leadership Statistics from TeamStage show that 76% of people between 55–60 believe men and women can lead equally (Tina, 2023). Although women continue to face significant barriers on their path to the top, the data proves otherwise because there can and should be an inclusive and equitable future for women in leadership.

Let me take you back to a chilly winter morning when I sat at a conference table surrounded by the Executive Leadership Team (ELT). As one among three women and about six men in the room, I couldn't help but feel excitement and trepidation at this critical meeting. It was a forum to determine the fate of one of the most influential brands in our company, and I was ready to contribute my expertise and ideas as always.

As the discussion unfolded, I noticed a subtle shift in the room's dynamic. My male colleagues seemed to dismiss my suggestions. It was as if my voice was fading into the background, drowned out by the echoes of gender biases and outdated stereotypes.

Frustration began growing within me because I knew I had the skills, knowledge, and passion to make a significant impact, and my contributions needed to be more valued and noticed, but that wasn't the case.

These scenarios have ruffled many women's confidence through the years because, with such attitude in the workplace, they grapple with self-doubt and imposter syndrome, the byproducts of generations of gender biases in executive positions. The constant fear of failure and the belief that everyone is scrutinizing their every move cripples faith in their potential, stifling innovation and erasing the desire to push forth new ideas that propel companies forward. When you yearn for career advancement but struggle to find your purpose and navigate the path to success, it can leave you in doubt. Or when you crave support, collaboration, and a strong network to inspire and be inspired by others, knowing deep down that you have the qualities necessary to lead if only you're given a chance, but no one notices, it isn't very encouraging.

Globally, more women encounter a lack of training and exclusion from meaningful decision-making processes, leaving them feeling the weight of gender inequality in their professional lives. In fact, some colleagues and leaders aged 35 to 54 still cling to archaic gender biases, resulting in men passing women over for promotions, being demoted, or receiving unequal pay compared to their male counterparts (Greenwood, 2023).

Furthermore, women seeking leadership positions battle insecurities that prevent them from speaking up and sharing their brilliant ideas. The fear of being unheard or dismissed prevents you from contributing innovative perspectives and creative wisdom. You may not fully develop your emotional intelligence to face the challenges ahead, so instead of trying, you remain silent while others move along in their careers. On top of it, another struggle of balancing work and personal life becomes ongoing when you try to nurture relationships and maintain a sense of self amidst the demands of your career. The weight of these competing priorities can take its toll, leaving you searching for a better way to achieve the elusive work-life balance.

The good news is, despite the myriad of strains, and worrisome statistics provided earlier, there is hope.

This book is a beacon of light for women seeking to transcend the obstacles and limitations imposed upon them by societal stereotypes. Within these pages, you will discover the tools, strategies, and insights to overcome self-doubt, shatter those brick walls of low self-esteem, and become a fearless female leader. You need to rewrite the narrative and redefine what it means to lead, starting with understanding who you are and where your success story begins. Rise above the limitations, embrace your full potential, and create a future where you and more women who aim for quality leadership are no longer the exceptions but the new narrative.

To achieve all of this, there are nine strategies you need to hinge on in this book because, with it, you will:

1. Learn to lead with authenticity and build trust with those around you.
2. Discover all the necessary soft skills, like empathy, adaptability, emotional intelligence, and optimism, to effectively lead teams and traverse different life hassles.
3. Master the art of communication and interpersonal relationships, which involves becoming a great listener, a persuasive speaker, and a non-verbal communicator.
4. Become a risk-taker, well-prepared to make calculated decisions that push you and your team toward success.

5. Collaborate more and work assiduously with any team to leverage the strengths of each team member and achieve shared goals.
6. Develop a leadership style that aligns with your personality and values while effectively achieving results.
7. Adopt a growth mindset to embrace challenges as opportunities for learning and expanding ideas.
8. Find your why—the driving force behind your leadership journey —to stay motivated and focused on your goals.
9. Arrive at the core of your journey by being the fearless female leader, leaving a lasting legacy for future generations of women hungry to make a difference.

That's the desired end this book is sure to provide. I know this because I am the first recipient of these benefits. It took me over 20 years to grasp and implement my leadership qualities for maximum success, and believe it or not, these strategies were my guide.

Once you follow these steps committedly, it will create a new difference to evolve a new you.

- You will embrace a life free from the fear of failure, turning it into boundless opportunities.
- Sudden steadfast confidence will emerge. One that will prepare you to take steps you dreaded in the past.
- You will become assertive and foster innovative teamwork that inspires others to excel.
- Life won't be about surviving but living, as you will achieve a harmonious balance between work and life.
- You will get a revamp in your growth mindset.
- The career path you seek will be propelled to unimaginable heights.

This transformative journey will continue as you internalize the principles in this book and make it the key to an evolving career.

Before I acquired the knowledge and insights I am sharing in this book, my journey toward becoming a fearless female leader was riddled with many challenges. As a 43-year-old married woman with two kids in the bustling New York metropolitan area, I faced the demanding pressures of balancing family responsibilities and pursuing a successful career.

For two decades, I navigated various leadership roles in boutique agencies, small businesses, and large organizations. While I experienced many victories and accomplishments, I also encountered setbacks and made mistakes. Through these trials and triumphs, I gained invaluable wisdom and discovered what it truly takes to be a fearless leader.

I struggled with self-doubt and uncertainty without the guidance and insights I possess today. I questioned my abilities and feared the consequences of failure. The lack of a roadmap to success left me overwhelmed and unsure, but I overcame these obstacles and emerged as a confident and empowered leader.

Armed with the lessons learned from my experiences, I am passionate about sharing this "new" information with you. I want to save you from the pitfalls and challenges I faced and provide you with the tools, strategies, and mindset needed to encounter the complexities of leadership fearlessness with grace.

I am excited to reveal the insights that will take you closer to your goals and enable you to create a lasting impact as a fearless female leader. Will the journey be difficult? Of course, however, the knowledge and guidance within these pages will equip you to overcome any obstacle and emerge as a winner—the confident, influential leader you were always born to be.

You picked up this book, so you're ready to embrace your authority, unshackle your true potential, and rewrite the rules of female leadership. It's time for women to step into their power and create a future where gender equality is not just a dream but a reality. Let's make a lasting impact and shape a world where women's voices are heard, respected, and celebrated.

CHAPTER I

THE POWER OF AUTHENTICITY

We must have the courage to embrace our true selves, even if it feels daunting or unfamiliar. —May Sarton (*Authenticity Quotes (1309 Quotes)*, n.d.)

It may sound unbelievable, but for most women, striving over the years to create relevance for themselves and their work hasn't been an easy journey. While most break their backs to be heard and seen, the BBC's 2022 Equality Matters issue confirms that 40% of women worldwide are in the workforce, 23% are CEOs, and 29% are fortunate to hold senior management roles (Bishop, 2022). This may look good considering the numbers; however, it's troubling all thanks to the boggling fact that most women who possess enormous potential and seek the perfect space to showcase their abilities to work, lead, and deliver are plagued with the reality of gender discrimination.

Gender discrimination is no longer a topic of concern for the United Nations or gender-based organizations to discuss and continuously evaluate; it's become a horrid reality that's shutting down women's opportunities to be their authentic selves, especially in the workplace.

WHAT IS AUTHENTICITY?

Authenticity for any female leader is about being honest, embracing her genuine self, and never apologizing for what she represents. Genuineness brings fearlessness because your focus starts getting better at what you're good at until you're labeled the game-changer in the leadership.

The New York Times publication and a host of research could confirm that women make the most profitable decisions at the most stressful times in the workplace. It pinpoints that the success rate of women heading business affairs and driving organizations is far more outstanding irrespective of the demands of climbing the ladder.

The authenticity of female leaders is necessary to empower them to break bounds, defy societal odds, and stay true to themselves and their cause. It begins from within and transcends into their respective roles in their personal lives and professional environment.

Authenticity in the Workplace

Authenticity for women is their ticket to building trust in the industry they represent. Once you decide to be different, unique, and exceptional, you create for yourself the golden opportunity to unlock the business' success and other benefits.

So, a good workplace must meet specific criteria for authenticity to come into plain sight so that women can be felt, heard, and seen like their male colleagues:

1. **Trustworthiness:** It should set women apart as genuine and trustworthy individuals that work hard and are credible enough to deliver and sustain profitable relationships with colleagues, clients, and stakeholders. Their authenticity is about trust, sincerity, and commitment to work and deliver, which will breed support and stronger connections.
2. **Diversity, equity, and inclusion (DEI):** With authenticity comes workplace diversity, equity, and inclusion (DEI). Anyone who can embrace their true identity sets the stage for an environment that appreciates values and respects diverse perspectives, experiences, and identities. Feeling safe to be

yourself cultivates a working culture of acceptance and belonging, where individuals can contribute their unique talents and ideas. Women need this to thrive in their career path as it will give them bold, opinionated, and brave confidence in role execution.

3. **Integrity:** Authenticity aligns actions with core values. Stay true to your beliefs, principles, and all you stand for pushes you to make congruent decisions with who you are. A female leader with this quality will feel fulfilled and inspire others around you. Leaders who lead with integrity pay close attention to how they present themselves to others, and in doing so, they inspire trust, loyalty, and respect, and it positively impacts team members in organizations.

4. **Innovation and creativity:** Authenticity also promotes innovation and creativity. Bringing your genuine self to work helps you tap into your unique perspectives and talents, and, at this point, your innovative thinking is revealed and encouraged. Nothing is more attractive than a female leader who knows her opinions and can share fresh ideas irrespective of the outcome. Even when they think you don't have it, show them that you're bursting with creativity, and you won't stop until they see what's there, ingenuity.

5. **Supportive work environment:** Authenticity in the workplace should spawn a high level of well-being and job satisfaction. When you know you can be yourself at work, the chances are you'll work passionately because not only are your feelings considered, but your career growth is just as significant to you as it is to your team and supervisors, which is refreshing. It allows you to find meaning and purpose in your work, leading to higher engagement and productivity. That way, there is no room for burnout which over 60% of women experience before they hit 40 (Weller et al., 2021). The stakes are high in their journey to discover themselves as mothers, career women, and female leaders, so they try to do too much to stand out. But, with attention to authenticity, they own the stage by creating a work environment that supports women's well-being and meets their job satisfaction.

How to Be Authentic?

For a female leader to be fierce in her leadership role and show authenticity in the execution of it, the following points are to be kept in mind:

- **Identifying your skills:** What are your strengths and weaknesses, and how can you release a mind-blowing conversion rate? Once you understand your qualities, your role will be easy to maneuver because your confidence and communication ability will cascade.
- **Networking:** In the workplace and as an entrepreneur, recognizing your brand and establishing a strong network that empowers you to showcase your expertise is paramount. In my years of working, the power of networking was the one thing I never took for granted as I began to understand myself in the workplace. It gave me the professional identity I needed to stand out because I let engagement and excellent interpersonal relations guide my journey. The cornerstone of my success was based on my adeptness in networking and cultivating meaningful connections, serving as catalysts for expediting work completion. That credibility and strong relationships you make will always single you out as authentic and lead you into the hands of people who are transparent in their actions and accountable for their transactions.
- **Continuous learning and growth:** Suppose you're shying away from grand opportunities to shine and showcase your capabilities. In that case, it's time you change everything because continuous learning and growth are about investing in yourself by converting mistakes into prospects and achievements.

A fearless leader must always be eager to sell herself through her work, values, and achievements. How will they know you matter in the workplace if you don't show your skills to them?

Make them see your true self and appreciate your exceptionalism because it always comes back rewarding in the long term.

Once you start in that manner, you can be like Mindy. Initially, she struggled with confidence in the workplace, doubting her abilities and fearing judgment. But a spark ignited within her one day, and she encountered stories of fearless women who overcame similar challenges. Determined to find her authentic voice, Mindy sought supportive mentors, attended workshops, and connected with empowering women. Slowly, her confidence grew, and she realized she had unique strengths to offer. With newfound passion and authenticity, Mindy became committed to sharing her ideas and earning respect from colleagues. She became a beacon of inspiration, empowering others to embrace their power. Mindy's journey showcased the transformative power of authenticity, passion, empathy, and optimism, proving that confidence can be cultivated and dreams can be achieved.

But, to get to where she did, there are strategies that every female leader must apply and imbibe:

1. **Personal development and internal growth:** Start investing in yourself and focusing more on personal growth. Don't be stuck in the mud and expect to create relevance; connect more through workshops, courses, or self-reflection on delivering your ideas better. Once you build a supportive network, you keep evolving until you get to that place where you become the best version of yourself. A personality people will enjoy working with and learning from.

2. **Establish psychological safety for yourself and others:** To stay real, vulnerable, and honest, there must be a safe space to encourage open communication, active listening, and support for each other's ideas and challenges. This shouldn't be missed, as it is the warehouse for successful leadership and performance output. Valuable, diverse perspectives promote open communications and collaborations that motivate colleagues and team members to contribute and get the best work done.

3. **Be vulnerable; it's your superpower:** There is nothing wrong with showing weakness sometimes. Embrace your unique quirks and imperfections because you are showing you are yourself; believe it or not, magic always comes with it. You get to reveal yourself without realizing openness was all it took. When Brene Brown, the American Professor, gave a TED Talk on Vulnerability,

she affirmed that it was the gateway to building trust and stronger connections. Share your passions, values, and journey with your work community. They get to see the real you and connect on a deeper level.

4. **Power up using feedback:** It's your secret weapon to getting honest, constructive criticism that will help you improve and revamp. A leader must never fear how people judge them or their work. There can be no growth there because if people have nothing good or bad to say about you or your work, then there is blandness in your existence. Feedback helps the woman understand her strengths, recognize her blind spots, and refine her leadership style.

5. **Sustain authentic connections:** Build genuine relationships within and outside the workplace. Connect with people who inspire you, share your values, and lift you. It starts by listening keenly without any sense of judgment or conclusions but just being present and showing that respect for opinions and others' perspectives. Authentic connections are pure gold!

6. **Hold firm to strengths and weaknesses:** There is a lot to gain from identifying your strong and weak sides. Learn from them, use them, and when you're surrounding yourself with a team that compliments you, pay attention to how these characters in you can come to play. According to recent studies from Gallup, if a person can get emotionally and psychologically prepared for anything, they will become productive and thrive in their leadership role because they comprehend the science of feelings.

7. **Learn to be a value-driven leader:** Lead with your heart, define your core values, and let them guide your decisions and actions. Be true to yourself, and the journey will be even more fulfilling.

8. **Accept mistakes as stepping stones:** We all mess up sometimes, and that's okay! Embrace your mistakes, be transparent about them, and learn from them. It's all part of being human and authentic.

9. **Practice self-love and self-care:** You're a fearless leader, and as a woman, you need self-care. Prioritize yourself, always. As crucial

as your career goals might be, take time for self-care, recharge your energy, and give yourself some affection.

ENCOURAGE AUTHENTICITY

Many people don't admit it, but caring for yourself makes you confident enough to speak freely about anything. Nothing scares you as much because you've grown, and now, you're ready to help other individuals find themselves on their path to authentic leadership. You can encourage authenticity in the following ways:

1. Lead by example: Remember, you're being watched; everything you do can inspire or dispel others in their decisions. So, lead by example; you could guide and inspire thousands. Your every action, inaction, or interaction is a significant determinant of how people respond to issues and their decision to be genuinely transparent in making authenticity their watchword. Your exemplary life is their execution model.

2. Inclusive leadership: Inclusive leadership is another vital aspect of encouraging authenticity. Create a safe and welcoming space where everyone's voices are heard and valued. Embrace diverse perspectives and encourage open dialogue where conversations and inhibitions are pronounced without fear or reservations. When people feel included and accepted, they are more likely to feel comfortable expressing their true selves.

3. Promote authenticity: Authenticity should extend beyond your behavior and into your products and services. Promoting authenticity by aligning your offerings with your core values is crucial for an entrepreneur. Don't sell something you wouldn't personally buy to prove you have the power to do so. Let your products and services reflect your respect for authenticity, and customers will appreciate your integrity.

4. Share your story: Additionally, sharing your own story and successes can be incredibly empowering. Regardless of how small or big your achievements may seem, they demonstrate that authenticity leads to positive outcomes. Being vulnerable and

open about your journey inspires others to embrace their unique paths and take pride in their accomplishments. Kamala Harris is one woman who, through her autobiography, "The Truths We Hold: An American Journey," spoke openly about her political career and the hurdles she crossed to reach her destination. Today, her story empowers women to know they can break barriers and reach their leadership expectations once they are determined and focused.

5. Build authentic connections: Remember to mix business and pleasure when necessary. Building authentic relationships means showing genuine interest in others as individuals, not just as colleagues or clients. Find common ground, share personal anecdotes, and foster a sense of team spiritedness that makes integrating work-life balance swift and exciting. Trust and authenticity naturally follow when people feel a personal connection, along with job satisfaction that will make people appreciate the leadership and not assume they must abandon themselves for service.

6. Transparency: In your marketing efforts, focus on responsible messaging and transparency—market responsibly by delivering unbiased and accurate information to your audience. Don't make promises you can't keep or misrepresent your products or services. Authenticity in marketing builds trust and loyalty among customers.

7. Consistency: Consistency is vital to promoting authenticity. Be consistent in your words, actions, and values. Inconsistency breeds confusion and erodes trust. When you consistently align your behavior with your beliefs, people will see you as dependable and trustworthy.

8. Accountability: Being responsive and accountable is essential for fostering authenticity. Give people the attention and support they deserve; respond promptly to inquiries, feedback, and concerns; take ownership of your mistakes and learn from them. Accountability demonstrates integrity and a commitment to doing what's right no matter the eventuality.

SEGUE

Besides these tips, most importantly, recognize that the key takeaway for every female leader is to understand that authenticity begins and ends with being true to self and empowering others. Once you pursue your goals both ways, the potential for success is limitless.

CHAPTER 2
EMOTIONAL INTELLIGENCE

Emotional intelligence is the innate power within us, a force that transcends the tangible. It empowers us to skillfully navigate the depths of human behavior, effortlessly embrace social complexities, and consciously make authentic choices that manifest remarkable outcomes. —Travis Bradbury (Lonczak, 2023)

In climbing the ladder of becoming a successful leader, you can leave nothing to chance. Once there, many things are expected of you, but most importantly, your ability to overcome hurdles and manage situations will assure your team about the future. Hence, the approach begins with how you respond to the different emotional displays that arise from encounters, confrontations, and networking. There must be a proper way to balance it all and stay ahead as a unique leader. That's where emotional intelligence comes up.

Let's understand the above said with an instance from my professional journey: In a challenging scenario between myself and my team members, we faced a crucial deadline for a Board of Directors meeting, where we were to present in front of top executives from our parent company in Japan and the esteemed ELT team. The pressure was mounting, causing stress levels to skyrocket and emotions to run high. With limited time to prepare our presentation, it was essential to impress them with the remarkable progress we had made since our last encounter. Recognizing the significance of this moment, I chose to lead with a more authentic and supportive approach, fostering a connection rather than resorting to a bossy or authoritative demeanor. I firmly believed that by embracing our collective strengths and nurturing a positive atmosphere, we could conquer any challenge and emerge victorious. We embarked on this crucial meeting with determination and optimism, ready to showcase our accomplishments and win hearts.

First, I listened to my team members to understand all their worries, and then in acknowledging their feelings, I validated their experiences. I didn't do it to get into their good books; I wanted to test how empathy would make them feel safe enough, to be honest in their opinions during the open dialogues. Although it all seemed chaotic, with so many views flying through the room, I still had to maintain calm and manage my emotions. This enabled me to facilitate constructive conversations, encouraging team members to collaborate, share perspectives, and find common ground.

My approach toward the situation inspired my team members; it gave them insight into the importance of emotional intelligence and how it had become a vital tool for any leader who wants their team to be productive. Statistics show that in research done by 80 scientists over 40 years, it was apparent that emotional intelligence is a more in-demand skill than technical as it provides satisfaction and ensures productivity.

WHAT IS EMOTIONAL INTELLIGENCE?

It isn't a scientific element but a skill that enables individuals to understand and manage their own emotions and the emotions of others. As a female leader, your ability to perceive and regulate emotions effectively and interpersonal interactions plays a crucial role in the workplace. With it, you can

- build strong relationships—by understanding and empathizing with the emotions of their team members, female leaders can foster positive relationships based on trust, respect, and collaboration. They can connect with others on an emotional level, which enhances communication and teamwork.

- make informed decisions—emotional intelligence enables female leaders to consider how their choices affect other individuals and teams. They can weigh different perspectives, manage conflicts constructively, and take steps to balance the organization's needs with their employees' well-being.
- inspire and motivate—female leaders with high emotional intelligence understand what drives and motivates individuals. How? Because they have spent much time watching people, listening to them, and connecting with them, they now recognize the struggles and desires people seek. It makes it easy for them to effectively communicate goals and expectations to resonate with their team's emotions and aspirations. Moreover, employees feel they can lean on their leaders for support and guidance as they aim to rise in the industry, making them the perfect role models.
- navigate challenges—with the resilience and adaptability to navigate challenges and setbacks, female leaders can have well-groomed emotional intelligence. While encountering difficult situations, they can hold their strength and support their team members enough to cope with stress and overcome obstacles. The ability to handle challenges comes with strategic confidence and stamina attained through a series of transitions and transformations.
- promote inclusive and positive work culture—this is the era of diversity and inclusion, and having a leader create a positive work environment; with this approach, only they can possess the emotional intelligence to ensure no one is left out in building a long-term fulfilling work culture. They are attuned to the emotional needs of their team members and promote a culture of empathy, psychological safety, and mutual support. This contributes to higher employee engagement, satisfaction, and overall well-being of the leader and the employees.

In the study by the renowned author Daniel Goleman, he presented pillars of emotional intelligence as signature characteristics of personality that are nurtured over time with self-study, discipline, and intentionality. He shared self-awareness, self-regulation, motivation, empathy, and social skills. They are the foundation of effective interpersonal relationships, communication, and organizational leadership, and further research shows that leaders with high emotional intelligence are more likely to inspire and positively influence their teams, leading to improved performance. A female leader who exudes finesse in the execution of responsibility and relationality with the masses proves the relevance and absorbability of emotional intelligence.

Let's discuss in deeper detail what these components represent:

1. **Self-awareness:** Recognizing one's emotions, strengths, weaknesses, values, and motivations. Self-awareness enables individuals to understand how their feelings influence their thoughts, behavior, and those around them. It is either an internal or external effect you experience from one of these behaviors; however, the inevitable fact is that being self-aware gives you the edge in the emotional intelligence approach as a leader.

2. **Self-regulation:** This component is about effective management. Any female leader who knows how to control their emotions, impulses, and reactions strategically, adapts to change and remains calm in challenging situations can rest assured that their authenticity will shine through their regulated sense of focus.

3. **Empathy:** It's about how you share in the emotions of others. As a boss, you have a peculiar case of a staff whose agreed shift affects their mental health and ability to work productively; how would you address it? Would you replace them in a snap because their sloppiness might cost you a multi-million-dollar contract, or would you share in their predicament by finding ways to mitigate the situation or at least reach a reasonable agreement? This is where the question of empathic leadership comes into play. It involves actively listening, observing non-verbal cues, and being able to put oneself in another person's shoes. Despite your role as a leader, empathy allows you to connect with others on an emotional level and respond compassionately.

4. **Social skills:** This encompasses a range of abilities related to effective communication, relationship building, and teamwork. This component involves communicating clearly, resolving conflicts, collaborating, and influencing others positively. Strong social skills facilitate healthy and productive relationships. Also, most studies reveal that social skills can assist your intuitive abilities. Your sense of prediction and foresight in reading people and situations strengthens and becomes more distinct because of your connections with people. Somehow, it's like you've seen a scenario play out several times and can tell how it might turn out, which gets you prepared, aware, and emotionally in control.

5. **Motivation:** It is the longing for a drive and enthusiasm to achieve personal and professional goals. It involves setting challenging goals, having a sense of purpose, and maintaining optimism even in the face of obstacles. Motivated individuals are resilient and proactive in pursuing their aspirations.

According to research conducted by Future Talent Learning, emotional intelligence matters in leadership due to its ability to positively influence strategy and decision-making. Leaders with vital emotional intelligence can effectively navigate complex situations, adapt to change, and make informed choices considering organizational and employee well-being. This promotes a supportive and inclusive work environment, fostering engagement and satisfaction.

How to Manifest Emotional Intelligence?

So, how does emotional intelligence manifest? It involves communicating assertively, resolving conflicts constructively, and handling stressful situations with composure. Once these are in place, an organizational system will work effectively. Any leader who aims to attain all these characteristics and more for the latter to thrive can do it, but it comes with a learning process. Once you can identify the tips for becoming emotionally intelligent enough to create a functional and personal empire, the next step is to use them at every chance.

The nine golden tips to becoming emotionally intelligent are:

1. **Communicate:** Being authentic is clearly communicating your emotions to your employees. Let them comprehend what you don't say and what you do at any given opportunity. It makes the environment move coordinately because your team can make decisions based on their understanding of your emotional dispositions. They have worked with you over time and can tell the best-suited approach to any situation, irrespective of your absence or presence.

2. **Self-reflection:** In nurturing emotional intelligence, knowing, understanding, and reading self is critical; that way, people connect with you easily. It exudes authenticity if you take the time to self-reflect and be aware of who you are and what you represent regarding emotions, strengths, weaknesses, and focus. The impact on others is profound as they absorb your character; they can see you achieving synchronization in working output.

3. **Be attentive:** When you genuinely desire to test your emotional reading capacity, set up meetings, workshops, and gatherings and assess the passion level of individuals. Yes, it's a working environment, but that doesn't mean it's not open to having an emotional atmosphere of disagreements, sentiments, and indifference. As long as you deal with humans, it's bound to come up, and an emotionally intelligent leader can listen attentively, observe the tempo of the discussions, and make decisions that would meet everyone halfway. As a result, they would feel heard, appreciated, and valued.

4. **Be imaginative:** Many people would advise you to put yourself in their shoes; that's hard, considering no one knows how tight or loose the other's shoes are. I always say to keep your imagination broad to help you see things from a realistic perspective. If you, a male CEO, get an employee report on your desk every other week about a sickly pregnant lady due to her falling behind on her projects, you won't be able to put yourself in her shoes (we know why); however, if you imagine having a wife, working her heart out to be valued despite her condition, then you'll learn how to show empathy to the plight of a pregnant employee whose trying her best to work hard. Emotional intelligence makes you a person of

compassion and support to your employees, which automatically means work success.

5. **Encourage collaboration:** Create an environment where you don't have this massive gap between you as the leader and your employees. As often as possible, teamwork must be so everyone feels valued and needed. With collaboration comes diverse perspectives where individuals are empowered to contribute their unique strengths and be open about their weaknesses, so everyone compliments each other to maximize profit.

6. **Show passion and optimism:** Enthusiasm, dedication, and positivity for your work can inspire your team to share your passion and strive for excellence. Passionate leadership motivates and energizes those around you, sending a vibe whenever you are present. Even if employees are going to do overtime, they'll do it happily, knowing they have a leader who will ensure they are well compensated and stay supportive and optimistic through the entire tedious journey.

7. **Promote work-life balance:** Recognize the importance of well-being and support your team members in achieving a healthy work-life balance. Give them time off and flexible schedules and provide resources for managing stress like a small game room, a short nap corner, or even a monthly happy hour where employees can get together to unwind and share stories; it bonds colleagues with their bosses and creates a whole new network of interpersonal relationships, a vital tenet of emotional intelligence.

8. **Lead by example:** Model the behaviors and values you expect from your team. They will know the expected standards once you show integrity, fairness, and ethical conduct while establishing trust and respect. Nothing more, nothing less. As a woman who hungered to get on the best side of my colleagues and one day be my own boss, I always aimed to lead by example, and for me, it was about taking responsibility for my mistakes and admitting when I was wrong. I wanted people around me to tell me my weak points, and the moment I showed that vulnerability, it fostered an environment of accountability, growth, and freedom.

9. **Make informed decisions:** A lot weighs on the shoulders of most leaders. In the case of a female leader who tries to make her

employees respect her role and appreciate her contribution, it can be even more demanding. However, the rule doesn't change but upgrades. Her decisions in any case presented must come from a place of emotional comprehension where she understands all sides and remains as firm as she can until the best outcome emerges. This tip is most important because it shows authenticity to lead in fairness and justice and not be prejudiced by any perspective.

HOW TO USE EMOTIONS WISELY

An essential characteristic of a successful leader is harnessing the opportunity to use emotions wisely to think profoundly and address issues smartly and strategically, so much so that most employees and individuals don't know what to expect. It's a skill born from being coherent, diplomatic, and output-driven.

Strategic Thinking and Problem-Solving

Strategic thinking is a skill that enables leaders to envision the future and develop an effective plan of action to achieve organizational goals. It involves considering long-term objectives by assessing any project's anticipated mission and vision, reviewing the possible pitfalls that could come up irrespective of how good the blueprint might look, and identifying growth opportunities. To do this successfully requires lots of data and resources from past and present for analysis to avoid being subjective in conclusions and critical in findings. Women leaders who are in touch with their emotions and understand the power of critical thinking often exhibit strong strategic abilities, as they have a clear vision and can navigate complex business landscapes.

To enhance strategic thinking skills, several approaches should be considered.

- Firstly, a deep understanding of the organization's purpose and values is essential. What are the company's mission, vision, goals, and traction plan? This clarity helps align decision-making with every other aspect of the company's desired goal.
- Secondly, effective strategic thinkers actively gather information, analyze trends, and seek diverse perspectives to make informed

decisions. They can anticipate potential obstacles and develop innovative solutions by considering multiple viewpoints. There must be a bi-vocal insight into everything to see the big picture.

- Thirdly, they are future-oriented and embrace a growth mindset. They allow change and are willing to take calculated risks. This mindset will enable them to seize opportunities and adapt their approaches accordingly. A Forbes publication asserted that although women show more growth and output mindset than men in the workplace, they are underrepresented in the role of CEO, and their strategic thinking capacity comes through later in life. This could be because their confidence level is affected, or the overwhelming drive to prove themselves sometimes takes away the focus to yield deep thinking. It's why cultivating strong communication and collaboration skills is essential for the effective strategic thinking of female leaders. Open dialogue and collaboration close unhealthy gaps and help leaders build consensus where their new ideas and valuable insights from others are combined and laid on the table to create what works for now and the future.

After years of rising in her previous role before becoming her own boss, a leading female CEO of a Consumer-Packaged Goods (CPG) company had this to say about the relevance of being strategic as a leader:

Strategic thinking stems from a deep knowledge of your business and the factors shaping your market, consumers, and suppliers. It goes beyond surface-level understanding and requires a detailed grasp of the processes driving your company. By delving into the specifics, you gain invaluable insights and prevent intermediaries from clouding your judgment. Understanding at a granular level empowers you to navigate political dynamics, avoid hidden agendas, and make informed decisions. Embracing this approach is essential for staying well-informed and effectively fulfilling your role.

Problem Solving

With strategic thinking, several tenets of leadership are met, from being organized, detail-oriented, and focused to becoming the best of all, a problem-solver.

People long to have leaders who can solve their problems, pay attention, and offer the best approach for everyone to leave the battlefield with a smile. Problem-solving is more than a talent but a critical leadership skill that empowers individuals to tackle challenges, make informed decisions, and drive positive organizational change. Successful women leaders demonstrate problem-solving skills when they combine analytical thinking with creativity and resourcefulness and approach problems with confidence, persistence, and an empathetic mindset. Care to know why? Well, a scientific angle is least explored where problem-solving is concerned between a man and a woman. In research conducted by Harvard in 2001, evidence showed that the frontal lobe and limbic cortex of the female brain, which was responsible for problem-solving responses and emotional conduct, were more prominent than in a male. This confirmed why women always show a higher sensitivity rate in handling issues. They tend to assess all persons and aim the best way possible not to hurt anyone. It's a compassionate reflection that can be fruitful but sometimes limiting when trying to satisfy everyone.

To effectively solve problems as a leader, a structured approach can be helpful. Once a problem presents itself, a leader mustn't try to prove their autonomy to make decisions, as this can turn out badly. There are steps to make the conclusion meaningful and authentic.

1. **Define:** Firstly, define the problem by looking at both sides to ensure a thorough understanding of the situation.
2. **Gather information:** Secondly, gather relevant information. Every circumstance happens with scenarios, facts, and figures that will be comprehensively analyzed. Suppose an employee comes with a complaint about a colleague or client. In that case, substantial evidence, data, feedback, and stakeholder perspectives must be used to measure and assess the gravity of truth or insinuation.

3. **Brainstorm:** Then comes the tricky part, brainstorming the right solutions. A study from an anonymous women's activist affirmed that because a woman possesses an empathic nature of paying attention to everyone's emotional behavior in any given situation, she tries to lay various solutions on the table. Considering all variables, she identifies a more encompassing approach, evaluating its feasibility, potential outcomes, and alignment with organizational goals. The minute all are checked, next comes effective implementation.

4. **Implement:** Implementing shows that communication and collaboration with stakeholders have been executed, and there is active support and engagement.

5. **Reflect:** Finally, reflect on the problem-solving process, identifying lessons learned and opportunities for growth. This reflective practice enhances future problem-solving abilities, so nothing is left to chance.

Confidence and Integrity

Confidence is a crucial characteristic of a fearless female leader. When you are confident, you trust your ability to make sound judgments and be bold in your decision-making which is an enormous inspiration to others. Confident leaders radiate self-assurance, instill trust, and motivate their teams to achieve greatness. Above all, when a woman exudes that stand-firm shoulder-high aura, it's one force to battle workplace discriminations which many women suffer.

How much belief do you have in yourself? Most leaders today came through successfully in their position either because they were surrounded by people who saw their potential and pushed them to take it a step further or were determined to beat the odds by shutting down the naysayers and focusing on bringing their dreams a step higher. It's never easy once you take the first step, but it's a lifetime of being brave and sure once you take a swing at it.

To cultivate confidence, there are various strategies to consider, and it can start with your outer body posture.

Stand Strong!

How do you stand when you're before people? Do you show your mental fear on the outside by looking downwards, scared, and a little withdrawn in your body language? That says a lot. To beat this, the first step is never to take every situation so seriously. Like Gabourey Sidibe, the American actress who would turn heads with her plus-size figure, would say, "One day I decided that I was beautiful, and so I carried out my life as if I was a beautiful girl." For her, as it should be for most people, once you care less about how people see and treat you and give your all to what's in front of you, the nerves slowly fade away, creating room for confidence to shine. Next, a growth mindset is essential, where challenges are seen as opportunities for learning and establishing. Successful women leaders understand that setbacks and failures are part of the journey and use them as stepping stones to future success.

Upgrade Yourself Always!

There always needs to be more knowledge to make you a perfect leader who has reached the peak of their career. No matter the amount of success amassed, a leader always aims to gain new ideas and be a step ahead of every new challenge. This comes with reading more innovative materials and listening to people and their opinions. You'll find it easy to come up with authentic ideas and share some of your own because you are well-informed and intellectually prepared to contribute to any discussion confidently.

Seek Feedback!

Seeking feedback and learning from others is another way to boost confidence. Actively seek mentorship or guidance from trusted individuals who can provide insights and support your growth. By embracing continuous learning and improvement, you develop new skills and expand your knowledge base, enhancing your confidence in your capabilities.

Attitude is Everything!

Maintaining a positive attitude and celebrating successes, no matter how small, shows you don't see things myopically. When you give yourself some credit by recognizing achievements and progress, you'll visualize success and set realistic goals confidently.

Focus on your objectives; it will take you to another comprehensive behavior and integrity character.

Be Transparent!

Here, a leader's moral principles are put into question. For a fearless female leader, it's about transparency, acting ethically in all circumstances, and upholding core values. These all seem tough; however, leaders who demonstrate integrity inspire trust, credibility, and loyalty from their teams and stakeholders. They are all about doing what's right regardless of what people say or the temptations that would try to spring them on a different path.

To lead with integrity, you must communicate honestly and transparently. Let employees see that openness in you when information is passed so they have no reason to suspect foul play or hidden agendas. Recent research proves that about 60% of female CEOs foster trust and transparency within their team as they don't hold back in the show of emotions (Tina, 2023). Although some may see this as a weakness, sensitivity is an asset to building integrity and winning your favor.

Be Accountable!

Another asset is being accountable for your actions, good or bad, and owning up to the outcome. When mistakes happen, be prepared to face the consequences rather than give excuses and play the victim. Demonstrate a willingness to learn, grow from the ordeal, move past it, and be ready to do better. One prominent rule customer service representatives hold firmly is, "Take the next available flight to get to the right destination." It just means that when you're trying to meet an angry customer's need, and they seem obstinate about their choices, take the subsequent wise decision of escalating the issue to your supervisor. It shows your commitment to job success and eagerness to improve when another situation arises. This authenticity and vulnerability foster a culture of integrity and continuous improvement.

Communication is the Gist!

Finally, promote open and respectful communication across boundaries where you have those moments when all your heart is in the right place, and you need to be hardcore in your decisions. It's normal and necessary that people feel fulfilled with leaders encouraging diverse perspectives, respecting all opinions, talking, and walking the walk.

Persistence, Determination, and Resilience

These are essential qualities of successful leaders, particularly for women navigating their careers and seeking to make a lasting impact in their respective fields.

To persist fuels the drive to keep going, even when faced with challenges. Staying steady on a course with an unwavering belief that with perseverance, anything is achievable, no matter the obstacles. Setbacks are the fuel that propels successful women leaders to soar even higher on their path to greatness. If you ever met a woman who rose without that personality that's persistent to the core, it's most unlikely. Persistence isn't a natural character; it's a learning mindset. Through continuous effort and a refusal to give up, anyone can pave the way for growth and accomplishment.

To enhance persistence, there are practical strategies to consider.

Clear Your Vision!

You need a clear vision of your goals and regularly remind yourself of your purpose. Suppose it has to become a mantra for you, perfect! The goal is to embrace a growth mindset, viewing challenges as opportunities that can take you to the groundbreaking level of your life. A review of great women like J.K Rowling, Martha Stewart, and Madam Walker will tell you that persistence always pays when you pay attention to the end product of your desire.

Seek Support!

Another thing, surround yourself with a supportive network of mentors and peers who inspire and uplift you to respond better to awkward circumstances. You can harness persistence and achieve remarkable results by staying focused, seeking support, and pushing through adversity which will build another noteworthy character of interest; determination.

Be Determined!

Determination is another crucial quality that propels fearless female leaders forward once they stamp their fit on the right course of action. It involves a tireless commitment, resilience, and the drive to persevere despite obstacles. Determined leaders have a clear sense of purpose and an unyielding belief in their abilities. They take decisive action, relentlessly pursue their goals, and inspire others with unwavering dedication.

To cultivate determination in your career, consider practical tips such as setting clear and specific goals, breaking them down into actionable steps, and tracking your progress. Surround yourself with positive influences and seek out role models who embody determination and inspire you. Embrace challenges as personal and professional growth opportunities, and celebrate even the smallest victories. By nurturing determination, you will forge your path with unwavering resolve and make a lasting impact.

Be Resilient!

Have you ever encountered a female leader who's so dogged about their beliefs and principles, whether it's appreciated or not? That's called Resilience. The ability to adapt, recover, and bounce back from adversity. Resilient leaders possess inner strength and the capacity to navigate change, setbacks, and stress gracefully. They maintain their composure, inspire their teams, and find innovative solutions to overcome challenges.

To become more resilient, focus on developing four core areas: physical, mental, emotional, and spiritual resilience. This involves caring for your physical well-being, fostering a positive mindset, building emotional intelligence, and connecting with a purpose. Practice self-care, seek support from your network, and embrace a growth mindset that views setbacks as opportunities for learning and growth. By nurturing resilience in all aspects of your life, you will become better equipped to handle the demands of leadership. You will see the roadmap of your goals before they come to life if you apply another powerful character trait—vision.

Visionary Thinking and Innovation

Visionary thinking and innovation are crucial for aspiring female leaders who want to impact their careers and industries significantly. By embracing the vision and fostering innovation, women leaders can drive positive change, create opportunities, and inspire those around them.

Having a clear vision provides a guiding light for leaders. It involves seeing beyond the present and envisioning a better future. Visionary leaders can articulate their goals, inspire others with their vision, and create a roadmap to achieve them. By communicating their vision effectively, they rally their teams and stakeholders, fostering a sense of purpose and direction.

To enhance your leadership vision, consider practical steps such as reflecting on your passions and values, researching industry trends, and seeking input from diverse perspectives. Continuously refine your vision based on feedback and new insights, and communicate it enthusiastically and clearly. By honing your vision, you can inspire others to join you on the journey toward success.

Innovation

Innovation is another vital skill that enables women leaders to think creatively, challenge the status quo, and drive meaningful change. It involves generating new ideas, taking calculated risks, and adapting to evolving circumstances. Innovative leaders embrace experimentation, encourage a learning culture, and foster an environment that values and nurtures creativity.

To foster innovation in your career, consider practical tips such as seeking diverse perspectives, cultivating a growth mindset, and embracing failure as a learning opportunity. Encourage open communication and collaboration within your team, and create space for brainstorming and idea-sharing. Embrace emerging technologies and stay informed about industry trends to identify opportunities for innovation. You can drive positive change and stand out as a leader by nurturing your innovative mindset.

Collaboration and Inspiration

In leadership, collaboration and inspiration are two essential pillars that empower female leaders to achieve remarkable success. By embracing collaboration, these leaders harness the power of teamwork, fostering an environment where diverse perspectives are valued, and collective achievements are celebrated. Additionally, female leaders uplift individuals and teams through their ability to inspire and motivate others, propelling them to surpass their potential. Let us explore these concepts further and discover how they contribute to the growth and empowerment of female leaders.

Collaboration is the cornerstone of effective leadership for successful women. They understand they can foster collaboration and tap into their teams' collective wisdom and diverse strengths. Embracing collaboration allows female leaders to create an inclusive environment where everyone's ideas are heard, respected, and valued. This enhances creativity and innovation and strengthens the bonds among team members. Collaboration enables women leaders to build strong relationships, encourage open communication, and create a sense of belonging within their teams.

Successful female leaders actively seek input from team members to excel in collaboration, recognizing that diverse perspectives lead to better decision-making. They establish clear goals and foster a culture of trust and respect, where individuals feel comfortable sharing their ideas and challenging the status quo. Effective verbal and nonverbal communication are crucial in collaboration, ensuring that messages are conveyed clearly, expectations are understood, and conflicts are resolved constructively.

By prioritizing collaboration, female leaders create an environment that cultivates teamwork, boosts productivity, and maximizes the potential of every individual.

In addition to collaboration, we have inspiration, a power tool for female leaders to employ to motivate and empower those around them and themselves. I often dissect inspire to mean "in" and "spite" where I chose to create the affirmation that:

- In spite of setbacks, I chose to move ahead.
- In spite of what my head might be telling me, my heart is in the right place.
- In spite of what people may conclude, it's not about them; it's the effort that counts.
- In spite of limitations, my eyes remain on the prize.

These affirmations may look casual, but they are for leaders to understand that inspiring others begins with firing up their authentic selves; then, they can ignite passion, drive, and a shared team vision. Through words, actions, and unwavering belief in their team members' abilities, they create a culture of positive energy, resilience, and continuous growth.

To inspire those around them, successful female leaders adopt various approaches. They lead by example, demonstrating integrity, authenticity, and a strong work ethic. By sharing their stories of challenges and triumphs, they create relatability and foster a supportive environment where everyone feels encouraged to pursue their dreams and aspirations. They provide guidance and mentorship, nurturing the talents and skills of their team members and helping them unlock their full potential. Celebrating achievements, no matter how small, inspires a sense of accomplishment and encourages individuals to set and reach ambitious goals.

Through collaboration and inspiration, female leaders have the power to transform workplaces, industries, and communities. They build bridges, break down barriers, and create a space where everyone's voices are heard and valued. In this collaborative and inspiring environment, individuals are empowered to unleash their creativity, take risks, and contribute their unique perspectives, leading to innovative solutions and extraordinary achievements.

As we embrace collaboration and inspiration, let us celebrate the achievements of successful female leaders who exemplify these qualities. The commitment to collaboration and their ability to inspire and motivate others serve as a guiding light, empowering women to break barriers, shatter glass ceilings, and lead purposefully. By embracing collaboration and inspiring others, female leaders pave the way for a future where everyone's potential can be realized, and gender equality and inclusivity thrive.

To Adapt and Sustain Inclusion

Adaptability is a key skill for aspiring female leaders who navigate the ever-changing landscape of today's professional world. Adaptability means embracing change, staying agile, and continuously learning and growing. It's about resilience in the face of challenges and seizing growth opportunities.

To cultivate adaptability as a leader, consider practical tips such as practicing mindfulness to stay present and focused, seeking diverse perspectives to leverage different ideas, and embracing new technologies and methodologies. Embrace a growth mindset that embraces change as an opportunity for personal and professional development. You can confidently navigate uncertainty and inspire others to embrace change by staying adaptable.

Inclusion is another vital skill for female leaders who seek to create diverse and inclusive environments where everyone feels valued and empowered. Inclusive leaders foster a sense of belonging and embrace diversity in all its forms. By actively seeking diverse perspectives, encouraging open dialogue, and creating an inclusive culture, they unlock the full potential of their teams and organizations.

To improve your inclusive skills, consider practical steps such as educating yourself about different cultures and experiences, actively seeking diverse perspectives, and addressing biases and microaggressions. Foster an environment where everyone's voices are heard and create opportunities for individuals to contribute and excel. By embracing inclusion, you can harness the collective power of diverse perspectives and develop a culture of belonging.

COMMUNICATE YOUR EMOTIONS SMARTLY

Are you trustworthy enough to communicate your emotions smartly?

Communication and trustworthiness are essential qualities for successful female leaders. Effective communication involves conveying information clearly, listening actively, asking insightful questions, and adapting your communication style to different audiences. It's about fostering open and transparent communication channels that promote collaboration and understanding.

Trustworthiness is the foundation of strong leadership. Trust is built through consistent actions, transparency, and integrity. Trustworthy leaders demonstrate reliability, keep promises, and act honestly and authentically. By building trust with colleagues, teammates, and employees, leaders create a supportive and productive work environment where people feel safe to take risks and contribute their best.

SEGUE

In developing essential soft skills, you must remember that character and emotional intelligence are the beginning of your journey as a leader. With tips for enhancing each skill, you're well on your way to delving deeper into the fundamental capabilities required for success. In the upcoming chapters, we will explore the power of effective communication—a necessary skill qualifying you to connect, inspire, and influence others with profound impact. Get ready to unlock the true potential of your leadership prowess in this transformative next step.

CHAPTER 3
THE ART OF COMMUNICATION

Communication - the human connection - is the key to personal and career success. —Paul J. Meyer. (Indeed Editorial Team, 2022)

L ike many other people, you've probably been in a position where your palms are sweating like crazy, and you can barely keep your legs together because all eyes are on you as you are making a speech. Well, it's not a new experience. In fact, amidst the organizational upheaval of the beverage company 'Jane' worked for, she found herself in a position where her team was demoralized, communication was strained, and there seemed to be a lack of direction. Recognizing the urgency to turn things around, 'Jane' persevered with determination despite the tension and uneasiness.

She gathered her team for a meeting, maintaining a calm demeanor; 'Jane' began by acknowledging their challenges and frustrations from the lack of effective communication. She then shared her vision for the team's success, articulating it clearly and inspiringly.

'Jane' observed her team members' non-verbal cues and reactions as she spoke, noticing their guarded expressions and hesitance to open up. Realizing that active listening was critical, she paused, inviting each person to share their thoughts and concerns.

'Jane' empathetically acknowledged the team's frustrations and validated their experiences. She listened to their feedback, addressing each concern with empathy and respect.

Every one of the tools she employed signifies the relevance of effective leadership communication. It's how you convey information, ideas, and goals'; or call it the clarity and compelling nature of creating influence using the right words and an appropriate emotional expression. It's the skillful use of verbal and non-verbal communication to inspire and motivate others towards a shared vision and see their work because your words have stuck to them. Once you can ensure clarity and conciseness without too much fluff, with empathy, understanding, and attentiveness, you'll have everyone seated to listen to your every word. When Oprah Winfrey shared her methods for effective communication, she put it down to one of many things; "have a conversation!" For her, there is no need to get all formal and serious to convey a message. Share stories and have a great laugh while you're at it.

TYPES OF COMMUNICATION

For successful execution, the different communication types and components representing them must be understood.

1. **Proactive communication:** It is an innovative method of communicating a compelling vision for the future. Influential leaders inspire and motivate their teams by clearly articulating a shared vision and the path to achieving it. They use vivid and persuasive language to engage their audience emotionally and intellectually. Leaders inspire team members to align their efforts and work towards a common goal by painting a compelling picture of the desired future state.

2. **Strategic communication:** It conveys strategies, goals, and plans to achieve organizational objectives. Leaders must communicate the organization's strategic direction, priorities, and milestones effectively to ensure everyone is aligned and working

towards the same goals. This type of communication involves clarity, specificity, and the ability to break down complex strategies into actionable steps. Effective leaders provide context, explain the rationale behind decisions, and guide their teams in understanding how their work contributes to the broader system.

3. **Inspirational communication:** It aims to motivate and energize individuals or teams. Successful leaders use storytelling, powerful anecdotes, and personal experiences to connect with their audience on an emotional level. They inspire others by sharing examples of success, perseverance, and the positive impact of their work. Inspirational communication creates a sense of purpose, builds morale, and fosters a belief in what is possible.

4. **Adaptive communication:** It is the ability to tailor one's communication style to different individuals, teams, or situations. Effective leaders understand that other people have unique preferences, communication styles, and information needs. They adapt their communication approach to ensure messages are understood and resonate with their audience. This includes using different modes of communication (verbal, written, and visual), adjusting the level of detail, and considering cultural or contextual factors.

COMPONENTS OF COMMUNICATION STYLE

Oral Communication

It refers to the spoken words and vocal delivery used by leaders to convey their messages. It includes face-to-face conversations, team meetings, presentations, and public speaking. Key aspects of effective oral communication for leaders include:

- **Clarity:** Leaders should articulate their thoughts clearly and concisely, using language that is easily understood by their audience.
- **Tone and delivery:** Leaders should pay attention to their tone of voice, emphasizing key points and using appropriate pauses and inflections to engage and captivate their listeners.

- **Active listening:** Leaders should actively listen to others, encouraging open dialogue and creating an environment where everyone feels heard and valued.

Written Communication

It is about using words to convey messages, instructions, reports, and other forms of written communication. Effective written communication for leaders includes:

- **Clarity and conciseness:** Leaders should express their ideas clearly and concisely in written documents to ensure the intended message is easily understood.
- **Structure and organization:** Leaders should organize their written communication logically and coherently, using headings, bullet points, and paragraphs to enhance readability.
- **Tone and style:** Leaders should adopt an appropriate tone and style that aligns with the purpose and audience of the written communication. They should maintain professionalism, clarity, and positivity.

Non-Verbal Communication

It involves body language, facial expressions, gestures, and other non-verbal cues. Effective non-verbal communication for leaders includes:

- **Eye contact:** Leaders should maintain appropriate eye contact to convey attentiveness and engagement.
- **Body language:** Leaders should know their body posture, gestures, and facial expressions, ensuring they project confidence, openness, and approachability.
- **Proximity and physical presence:** Leaders should be mindful of their physical presence and use appropriate proximity to convey accessibility and attentiveness.

Listening

It is a critical component of effective leadership communication. Leaders who actively listen demonstrate empathy, understanding, and respect for their team members. Effective listening for leaders includes:

- **Active engagement:** Leaders should be fully present and engaged when listening to others, giving their undivided attention, and focusing on the speaker's message.
- **Empathy:** Leaders should strive to understand the emotions and perspectives of the speaker, putting themselves in their shoes and responding with compassion.
- **Clarification and feedback:** Leaders should ask questions for clarification, paraphrase and summarize what they have heard to ensure understanding, and provide constructive feedback when appropriate.

A leader who commits to these components represents the authentic voice of the people. One famous American female leader who exemplifies effective leadership communication is Eleanor Roosevelt. As the longest-serving First Lady of the United States, she utilized her position to communicate effectively and advocate for social justice and human rights. She was meticulous in using words throughout her newspaper column, "My Day"; in her public speeches, she garnered support for her cause; on trips to communities, conversations were always crucial to her, and above all, she took advantage of the media to reach a broader audience to share in her fight for human right. She was an all-rounder and reflected on what future female leaders should promote.

Assessing her character and journey, it's safe to say that effective leadership has numerous benefits to the leader who desires to lead alongside their team.

BENEFITS OF EFFECTIVE COMMUNICATION

1. **Empowered and focused teams:** Effective communication provides clarity and direction, ensuring everyone, including you as a female leader, is on the same page. This empowers your team

members, enabling them to work towards common goals with confidence and focus.

2. **Trust and collaboration at the forefront:** As a female leader, you understand the importance of building trust and fostering collaboration. By actively listening to your team members, respecting their ideas, and encouraging open dialogue, you create an environment where everyone feels valued and included. This promotes stronger bonds and enables effective teamwork.

3. **Resolving conflicts with grace:** Conflict resolution is a crucial skill for any leader, and as a female leader, your ability to communicate effectively can bridge gaps and reach resolutions. By staying calm and respectful and considering different perspectives, you can facilitate constructive conversations that lead to ideal solutions, fostering harmony within your team and beyond.

4. **Nurturing customer relationships:** Strong communication skills are vital to building successful relationships with your team and customers. As a female leader, your attentive listening and clear explanations create customer rapport and trust. Understanding their needs allows you to provide tailored solutions and exceptional service, ensuring long-lasting customer loyalty.

5. **Aligning goals for success:** Aligning goals within your organization can be complex, but effective communication simplifies the process. By clearly conveying the organization's aspirations and objectives, you enable your employees, including other female leaders, to understand their roles and contributions. Regular communication builds trust, rapport, and a shared purpose, driving everyone toward common objectives.

6. **Minimized conflicts for a harmonious workplace:** Effective communication tactics help reduce conflicts or tensions within your team. Ensuring everyone receives the same information and clarifying expectations creates a fair and respectful environment where misunderstandings are minimized. This fosters a harmonious workplace where all team members, regardless of gender, feel heard and valued.

7. **Engaged and motivated employees:** Your communication skills connect and engage employees, leading to higher satisfaction and healthier company culture. By actively listening,

recognizing employees' skills, and fostering relationships, you empower your team members, including other women, to contribute fully and enjoy their work. This boosts morale and motivates them to perform at their best.

8. **Increased productivity and efficiency:** Effective communication gives employees, including fellow female leaders, a clear understanding of their roles and expectations. This clarity enables them to perform efficiently, leveraging their skills and resources effectively. By promoting open communication channels, you enhance productivity throughout the organization.

9. **Encouraging innovation and diverse perspectives:** Your commitment to open communication empowers employees to express their ideas and opinions, fostering innovation within the organization. You create an environment that encourages creative thinking and problem-solving by valuing diverse perspectives, including those of other female leaders. This approach drives continuous improvement and fuels the organization's success.

10. **Building strong and cohesive teams:** Effective communication strengthens team bonds and promotes trust among team members. You create a synchronized and supportive work environment by providing clear direction, setting guidelines, and ensuring everyone is on the same page. This cohesive teamwork, including collaboration with other female leaders, elevates the organization and leaves a positive impression on the public.

ACTIVE LISTENING—AN IMPORTANT COMMUNICATION RULE

When someone asks, "What are the leadership communication rules to help evolve a fearless female leader?" I say—active listening.

Why? The following are the benefits of active listening in leadership:

1. Active listening empowers female leaders to enhance business communication within the organization. Female leaders foster clear and effective communication by genuinely engaging with team members, colleagues, and stakeholders, driving better decision-making and overall outcomes.

2. Female leaders who can absorb information become role models for their teams, nurturing effective communication skills. By valuing diverse perspectives and encouraging open dialogue, female leaders inspire a culture of trust where everyone feels valued and empowered to share their ideas and concerns.

3. Attentiveness by female leaders creates a supportive environment, boosting employee morale and engagement. When employees feel heard and understood, job satisfaction increases, improving productivity and loyalty.

4. Female leaders build strong connections with their team members by having a keen hearing, reducing turnover rates. By valuing their opinions and contributions, female leaders foster loyalty and commitment, creating an environment where employees feel supported and motivated to stay.

5. Noting important information equips female leaders with conflict-resolution skills. By attentively listening and facilitating constructive dialogue, female leaders promote empathy and understanding, leading to more effective conflict resolution and a harmonious work environment.

6. It can empower employees, especially women, to express their unique perspectives. Female leaders create an inclusive space where diverse voices are valued, fostering collaboration, respect, and innovation.

7. Female leaders who pay close attention, encourage exploring new ideas and possibilities. By seeking diverse opinions and being open to different perspectives, female leaders foster better decision-making, innovative solutions, and a culture of continuous learning.

Challenges to Active Listening Skills

- **Distractions:** Noise, interruptions, or multitasking can make concentrating and actively listening to others challenging. Female leaders may face these distractions in various work settings, but being mindful of the importance of focused listening can help overcome this challenge.

- **Preconceived assumptions:** Bias or having a predisposition can hinder effective listening. Female leaders should be aware of their preferences and strive to approach conversations openly, suspending judgment and actively seeking to understand different perspectives.
- **Time constraints:** Busy schedules and tight deadlines often create time constraints for female leaders. Limited time may lead to rushed conversations, where listening takes a backseat. Overcoming this challenge requires prioritizing active listening and allocating dedicated time for meaningful conversations.
- **Emotional barriers:** Strong emotions, such as stress, frustration, or personal biases, can impede effective listening. Leaders should be aware of their feelings and strive to manage them during conversations, allowing for a more empathetic and objective listening experience.
- **Lack of empathy:** There can hardly be any meaningful conversation without traces of empathy. Female leaders may face challenges in empathizing with diverse perspectives or experiences. Therefore, it is essential to cultivate compassion actively, practice active listening to understand, and connect with others on a deeper level.
- **Information overload:** In today's fast-paced world, female leaders occasionally encounter information booms from several sources, making it difficult to process and retain as much data as possible while listening. Employing techniques such as summarizing key points, taking notes, or seeking clarification can help manage this challenge and ensure adequate comprehension.
- **Communication styles and cultural differences:** How you relate with people based on your cultural mannerism and roots can play a big part in how you receive information. As a leader, you should be sensitive to these differences and adapt your listening approach to actively bridge any gaps in understanding.

Why Does it Matter?

Effective listening is crucial because it allows us to understand others, build relationships, collaborate effectively, resolve conflicts, foster personal and professional growth, and enhance consumer satisfaction. When you listen attentively with a desire to comprehend

- you can grasp perspectives with interest.
- show the needed concern where helpful.
- integrate diverse ideas and find common ground.
- learn from others.
- meet consumer needs adequately.

It is a fundamental skill that promotes meaningful communication, connection, and positive outcomes in various aspects of life.

STRATEGIC STEPS TO EFFECTIVE LISTENING AND LEADERSHIP COMMUNICATION

1. **Be present:** Create a focused and conducive environment for communication, free from distractions. Give your full attention to the speaker, demonstrating active engagement.
2. **Practice empathy:** Seek to understand others' perspectives and emotions. Show genuine interest and concern, fostering a supportive and inclusive atmosphere.
3. **Suspend judgment:** Avoid making premature assumptions or forming opinions. Keep an open mind and listen without bias, valuing different viewpoints.
4. **Ask clarifying questions:** Seek clarity and a deeper understanding by asking relevant and thoughtful questions. This approach demonstrates your engagement and encourages the speaker to elaborate.
5. **Reflect and summarize:** Summarize the main points and reflect on the speaker to ensure accurate comprehension. This strategy reinforces understanding and validates their contribution.
6. **Provide feedback:** Offer constructive feedback and affirmations to the speaker, acknowledging their ideas and input. This tactic encourages continued participation and fosters a positive communication dynamic.
7. **Adapt communication style:** Tailor your communication approach to meet different individuals' and situations' needs and

preferences. Flexibility in your communication style promotes effective understanding and rapport.

8. **Encourage participation:** Create an inclusive environment where individuals feel safe to express their opinions and perspectives. Actively encourage and value contributions from all team members.

9. **Practice active listening:** Demonstrate active listening through nonverbal cues, such as maintaining eye contact, nodding, and using appropriate body language. Show that you are fully present and engaged in the conversation.

10. **Continuously improve:** Cultivate a continuous learning mindset and improve your communication and listening skills. Seek feedback, reflect on your performance, and actively work towards enhancing your leadership communication abilities.

SEGUE

Communication is the cornerstone of fearless leadership, elevating your impact from valuable to invaluable. Embrace the continuous improvement of your communication skills with every individual in your working environment, forging connections that empower and inspire. Through active listening, empathy, and open dialogue, create a safe space where diverse perspectives are celebrated and valued. As you cultivate this environment, you will overcome challenges and unlock the art of risk-taking. In the next chapter, we will explore the strategies to embrace calculated risks confidently, enabling you to lead with unwavering courage and embrace the transformative journey of fearless leadership.

CHAPTER 4
THE ROLE OF RISK-TAKING

If you take no risks, you will suffer no defeats. If you take no risks, you will win no victories. —Richard M. Nixon (*Risks Quotes*, n.d.)

Recent research states that one reason most people avoid taking risks is not because they can't but because of the fear of failing (LinkedIn, n.d.). Remember the word "fear"? An annoying little voice in your head constantly whispering, "*Watch out! Something bad might happen!*" But let me tell you, giving in to fear won't get you anywhere. It'll keep you stuck in your comfort zone, missing out on incredible opportunities and driving yourself crazy with "what ifs."

Now, let's talk about risks. They're like those thrilling roller coasters you're too scared to hop on. Sure, there's a chance you might scream your head off or feel a little queasy, but hey, that's part of the adventure! Taking risks propels us forward, pushing us to grow and discover our true potential. The legendary Helen Keller once said, "Life is either a daring adventure or nothing at all." (*A Quote From the Open Door*, n.d.)

Sure, it's totally normal to feel some fear when faced with risks. But here's the thing: fear shouldn't be calling the shots. You gotta look fear in the face and say, "*Not today, fear, not today!*" Trust me; you'll gain strength, confidence, and a kick-ass attitude by taking on those challenges head-on. As our buddy Mark Zuckerberg wisely said, "The biggest risk is not taking any risk. In a world that's changing fast, the only strategy guaranteed to fail is not taking risks." (*Mark Zuckerberg Quotes*, n.d.)

As a leader desiring to make a difference, the important motto for you, after integrity, should be risk-taking. The world keeps changing daily, and every attentive and present leader must work with the times and find best practices to navigate any circumstance, no matter the complexity.

The need to take risks is an unending demand to help every leader connect with innovations and project growth that will skyrocket their companies and businesses to the next level. How will you gain access to big clients and projects if you're all about the comfort zone? Do you think your employees will think outside the box if they notice you always aim to play safe? Once you think through all this, you'll appreciate the essence of calculated risks as the path to success, getting ahead of competitors, learning adaptability in any scenario the economy presents, and motivating and inspiring your team and clients to keep trusting your ability to deliver and best of all, seizing grand opportunities to break bounds and give the company a competitive edge.

Remember, "calculated risks" means under no condition should you feel the need to be impulsive in taking risks without thinking things through. That's not being smart but showy on your ability to dive head-on without swimming. Calculated risks are thoughtful evaluations of the potential benefits and drawbacks before deciding. They mean never misusing your emotions to cloud your sense of judgment. No great leader ever got far that way; in fact, to take risks that count:

- Be aware and clear on the potential risks and rewards.
- Aim to be authentic and transparent in your dealings.
- Assess all options presented to you.
- Seek advice on the value to be gained from the risks.
- Above all, show an openness to learn, fail, and rise again.

In leadership, these modes can do wonders for you and your team in the future, achieving productivity.

One of the most significant characteristics of a great leader is their desire to take risks that count: no running and hiding. According to a Yale School of Management study, leaders who take risks are often rewarded, particularly in competitive environments. These rewards can come from increased recognition, career advancement, and financial gains (Georgeac, 2021).

When Steve Jobs, co-founder of Apple Inc., took a significant risk by introducing the iPod in 2001, he didn't know it would be the product revolutionizing the music industry. At that time, the market was dominated by CDs and portable cassette players, and people were content with that, not knowing there were even better ways to enjoy music. The iPod's success was uncertain. However, Jobs believed in the potential of digital music and took the calculated risk of introducing a new and innovative product. It paid off. The iPod became a game-changer and set the stage for Apple's future success.

As a leader, when you can see what no one else sees after doing the due diligence of weighing all the pros and cons, rest assured that you'll get the following:

- The confidence of those who depend on you.
- The commitment of those who work with you.
- The attention of those who might want to ignore you.
- The open doors of more significant projects will elevate you.

Now you see that taking calculated risks places you on a new level. But, it begins first and foremost by overcoming your fears. You must train your brain to act when necessary and leave room for doubt and negativity. Notice that to take calculated risks is to drive success and re-channel the attitude of fear. Try doing that in three steps:

1. Rather than dwelling on the fear of failure, let your mindset take a different direction and view it all as a learning opportunity. See failure as a natural part of growth and development where lessons are learned to prop yourself forward.

2. Never allow fear to paralyze you; channel it into motivation and determination. Use it as a catalyst for action, pushing yourself to step outside your comfort zone and take calculated risks.

3. Take baby steps and manageable risks that gradually build your confidence. Break down bigger goals into smaller milestones, allowing you to experience success. Celebrate these achievements, no matter how small, as they reinforce your ability to overcome fear, take action, and take even bigger risks in the future.

THE ALTERNATIVES

In addition, some alternatives can be considered on your journey to fighting the fear of failure. I recommend this most to women seeking to make a difference as fearless female leaders:

1. Identify and challenge any negative or self-limiting beliefs contributing to fear. Recognize that self-doubt is expected but not always rational. So, use the weapon that works for you to mold your mind. Practice positive affirmations, focus on your strengths, and celebrate your achievements. Remind yourself of your capabilities and the value you bring as a leader; that way, fear won't have its grip on you.

2. Cultivate a growth mindset that hinges on continuous learning and sees setbacks as opportunities for growth. There is no such thing as an insurmountable obstacle; that's what you need to tell yourself constantly when in doubt. Reframing failure as a chance to learn and improve, you can approach risks with a more optimistic and open mindset.

3. Foster an environment that values and celebrates diversity and inclusion. Encourage diverse perspectives, create opportunities for underrepresented voices to be heard, and support the development of women leaders. When leaders feel empowered and valued, it can help mitigate the fear that may arise from societal pressures and biases.

A study published in the Journal of Personality and Social Psychology found that individuals who overcome the fear of failure and take risks have higher self-esteem and life satisfaction. Knowing they didn't bail out at the last minute isn't only a comfort but a sign that, with a little effort, they can reduce the fear of failing and taking risks. Also, a better way can come in more strategic steps:

1. **See failure as a learning tool:** An opportunity for growth where you are, allows you to refine your strategies and approach for future success.

2. **View failure as a stepping stone to greatness:** Once you recall how many successful leaders have experienced failures, use their stories as catalysts for achieving extraordinary outcomes.

3. **Practice self-compassion:** Be kind to yourself when faced with setbacks; understand that taking risks is a courageous act that requires resilience and self-encouragement.

4. **Pencil down the benefits of past failures:** How have previous failures provided valuable lessons, insights, and experiences that have shaped your leadership skills and decision-making?

5. **Surround yourself with a supportive network:** Seek out mentors, colleagues, or a peer group that can provide guidance, encouragement, and a safe space to discuss challenges and bounce back from failures.

6. **Set realistic expectations:** Understand that taking risks involves uncertainties, setbacks, and the potential for significant rewards and growth. Align your expectations with the process of learning and improvement.

7. **Focus on small steps:** Break down significant risks into minor, manageable actions that can help build confidence and momentum. Celebrate each step forward, regardless of the outcome.

8. **Nurture a growth mindset:** Cultivate a philosophy that supports challenges and sees setbacks as opportunities for growth rather than fixed limitations or indicators of failure.

9. **Seek feedback and continuous improvement:** Actively seek feedback from trusted sources to gain insights into areas for improvement and refine your approach to future risks.

10. **A big cheer to your successes:** Acknowledge and celebrate your achievements and successful risk-taking endeavors,

recognizing the courage it took to step out of your comfort zone and make a positive impact.

It's a challenging but laudable choice. For instance, you leave the comfort of a job that pays well and ensures your financial security to pursue your passion in the hope of growth. That takes a lot of guts and planning. Informed decisions and taking calculated risks are imperative if your career and leadership passion is to see the light of day.

RISKS THAT COUNT

As a female leader desiring to be fearless and driven, **how do you take risks that count?**

- **Weigh your risk-taking capability:** Reflect and evaluate your past experiences with risk-taking, considering how your unique experiences as a female leader have shaped your risk appetite so far. You have the statistics, so only you can give the correct answer.
- **Give room for failure:** Never deny potential obstacles and setbacks their fair share of existence; they must come, like it or not. But developing contingency plans to mitigate risks and recognizing the power of resilience and adaptability as critical attributes of successful female leaders will help prepare you for everything.
- **Define clear goals:** What are your desired outcomes? What are your objectives for the risks you are considering? Ensuring they align with your vision as a leader and contribute to your long-term career growth and empowerment—this is what counts the most.
- **Identify strengths and weaknesses ahead:** Assess your skills, knowledge, and resources, considering the unique strengths and capabilities you bring to the table and leveraging them to make informed decisions about the risks you are willing to take.
- **What do you and others stand to benefit from:** Evaluate the potential positive impacts of the risk-taking on your career, team, and organization, recognize the potential for advancing gender

equality, break barriers, and inspire other aspiring female leaders. With this gain, the risk will be worth taking.

- **Seek guidance from experts:** Consult mentors, advisors, or successful female leaders who can provide valuable insights and perspectives specific to the challenges and opportunities women face in leadership roles, empowering you to make informed risk-taking decisions.
- **Get comfortable taking tiny risks at first:** Start with smaller, manageable risks to build confidence and gradually increase your risk tolerance, recognizing that taking calculated risks is an integral part of the journey towards achieving gender equality in leadership.
- **Be ready to adapt:** When you think about risk, think agility and flexibility because risk-taking often involves navigating through gender biases and stereotypes and being able to adjust your strategies and approaches to create positive change.
- **Be around like-minded people:** A supportive network of diverse female leaders and allies who share your passion for breaking barriers is an excellent way to support one another in taking risks. Most of all, it's a collective method to advance women's leadership.
- **Remember self-awareness:** Continuously reflect on your strengths, weaknesses, and the unique challenges female leaders face, using self-awareness as a tool for personal growth, resilience, and inspiring others through your journey.
- **Be diverse:** Diverse perspectives, ideas, and approaches should always be a welcome development. Be aware of the importance of inclusivity in decision-making and its positive impact on innovation, problem-solving, and driving positive change.
- **Be accountable:** Hold yourself responsible for your risk-taking endeavors and openly communicate your goals and aspirations as a female leader, inspiring others and creating a culture that encourages women's leadership and risk-taking.
- **Follow the 3 A's of risk-taking:**

1. Act decisively.
2. Assess the outcomes.

3. Adapt your strategies and approaches based on the lessons learned.

You should embody the resilience and determination needed to succeed as a female leader.

- **Fail, but get up and proceed:** If you've heard the saying "fail fast but rise faster," you'll know that failure shouldn't be an excuse to sit back and dwell on the "had I known." Failure should be your stepping stone for growth and improvement, as you have been provided valuable lessons, paving your way toward success as a resilient leader.
- **Be ready to innovate:** Cultivate a mindset of curiosity, creativity, and a willingness to challenge the status quo, seizing opportunities for innovation from taking calculated risks and driving positive change in your leadership journey.

SEGUE

Unleash your potential by overcoming fear and embracing change, innovation, and learning opportunities. Don't let fear rob you of victories; instead, seize potential opportunities and grow from the valuable lessons they offer. Did you know overcoming fear is crucial in developing practical collaboration skills? When you let go of fear, you become more open to working with others, sharing ideas, and embracing diverse perspectives. Now, let's shift our focus to enhancing your collaboration skills in the next chapter.

MAKE A DIFFERENCE WITH YOUR REVIEW AND UNLOCK THE POWER OF FEARLESS LEADERSHIP

"Great leaders don't set out to be a leader...they set out to make a difference. It's never about the role—it's about the goal."
- Anonymous

Leadership is not just about guiding others; it's about empowering them to make their mark. True leadership embodies generosity, vision, and the courage to pave paths that others will walk after you. And today, I am reaching out to you with a heartfelt request.

Can you empower someone today with just a few words?Someone who, like you once were, is eager to lead but uncertain where to start?

My mission is to foster fearless leadership across every industry, making the principles of effective and transformative leadership accessible to all. This mission drives every word I write. But to truly spread this message, I need your help to reach everyone who can benefit from this book.

Judgments are often passed based on first impressions, and for books, that means its cover and its reviews. So, here is my appeal on behalf of a budding leader you haven't met yet:
Would you please take a moment to leave a review for this book? Your review is a simple act that costs nothing and takes less than a minute, but it can profoundly impact another's career and life. Your words could help:

- Another team achieve synergy and success.
- Another manager inspire and uplift their staff.
- Another CEO innovate and steer their company through challenges.
- Another entrepreneur create impactful change.

- Another vision come to life.

Feeling good yet? To assist another leader in their journey, scan the QR code below to leave your review.

If helping a future leader excites you, you're exactly who I wrote this book for. Welcome to our community of changemakers.

I am thrilled to help you develop into the leader you're destined to be, faster and more effectively than you've imagined. You'll find invaluable tactics, lessons, and strategies in the upcoming chapters.

PS - Remember, when you offer something valuable, it increases your worth to others. If you believe this book could benefit another aspiring leader, consider sharing it. It's another great way to spread leadership and make a positive impact.

Your support is extremely important to me. Great things can happen from a small gesture!

Leaving a fair and honest review on Amazon would enable other women to know about this book giving them the tools and strategies needed for their leadership journey.

CHAPTER 5
FIGHT IMPOSTOR SYNDROME

Alone, we can do so little; together, we can do so much. —Hellen Keller (Conley, 2022)

Every good structure didn't just take building materials and the knowledge to bring it to life; it took the commitment and dedication of people who worked tirelessly until they saw a finished edifice. There are countless buildings like the Empire State Building in the United States, the Eiffel Tower in France, and the ancient Pyramids of Egypt. These monuments have survived centuries of historical changes. They are still a wonder in the world because of teamwork, the collaboration of efforts and ideas, and respect for each other's perspectives and contributions.

Today, these skills are among the most in-demand requirements for the world's transition to higher interconnectivity and effective leadership. To position yourself as one with authority not nurtured in isolated brilliance but with the encompassing effort of collaboration and teamwork, you must believe in and support the strength of being team-spirited on your journey.

Collaboration isn't just about people combining their ideas because it would look good together, like date matchmaking; it pays attention to views from different sources. Somehow, everyone on a team is heard, their contributions and opinions are checked side-by-side with the desired outcome, and a decision is made. This approach in recent studies has become paramount, especially as about 75% of U.S. workers acknowledge that collaboration is vital for effective leadership and the work environment to thrive. They feel strongly about it because a report from KPMG affirms that, once again, 75% of female executives across over 150 leading global organizations have suffered imposter syndrome at some point (Boskamp, 2023). It shows that the connection between these figures is profound, and collaborative skills can significantly influence the leadership outcome in several industries.

WHAT IS IMPOSTOR SYNDROME?

Where the phrase impostor syndrome is used, it's synonymous with doubt, second-guessing, laid-back and low esteem. Not only do you have the skills, but you're also excellent at what you do. Regardless, there is still a fear of letting your work shine, and more times than not, you feel like some scam who doesn't have what it takes to win those big clients or execute those high-powered jobs.

When you're starting up your own sole proprietary business, that tends to happen because it's you against thousands of other competitors in similar companies. So, your work doesn't only have to speak for you; it needs to stand out. And, although you achieve that status of being significant and relevant, you still feel undeserving of the recognition for some reason.

But, like most phenomena, imposter syndrome slowly manifests itself through the character of the victim in several ways:

- Being successful is never enough. Most leaders with impostor syndrome disorder are often labeled high-achievers because they don't believe success is enough to quantify good leadership. They are fixated on their goals and go all out to make it happen, even if it breaks them.

- Overworking is a part of life. There is no room for playtime in their world because somebody must do everything perfectly. Mistakes are often viewed as significant blunders, potentially indicative of incompetence. Leaders with this trait are difficult to relate to as their employees walk on eggshells around them.
- The most common problem is self-doubt. More often than ever, the belief is that one's work is too unworthy to find its place among exceptional work. Even when trusted sources credit it as unique and authentic, it never changes the mindset of self-torture and belittling of efforts.
- Praises are more like savage statements than acknowledgment. Sensitivity to what's being said and how it's said can be a contention. Already, discontentment with their work makes any praise or recognition sound like a savage way of ridiculing their skills. For a leader with a big ego, their pride can be wounded easily without much effort since the sensitive behavioral response is profound.

In essence, imposter syndrome begins inborn and grows to create a character that's overly sensitive and judgmental of themselves and those around them. Richard Patterson, an American author, is among the famous personalities with their fair share of imposter syndrome disorder. His statement on the phenomena was striking as he described it as a character within most confident professionals where they get anxious and over-zealous to succeed before they're perceived as deceptive and their skills fraudulent. For him, these weird feelings make the victim work extra hard to clear their name and protect their records. (Patterson, 2023)

ARCHETYPES OF IMPOSTER SYNDROME

Honestly, this reason justifies the essence of impostor syndrome. But, like a white lie, there is no right way to celebrate a character trait that makes you second-guess your capabilities. To understand it better and approach it strategically, psychologists have taken the time to undergo studies that will clarify the different archetypes of Impostor Syndrome.

1. **Perfectionist:** This personality is all about high standards for themselves. They get so anxious about how things will turn out and if their work will be labeled as crap, regardless of their accomplishments. Good is never enough, except it's great.

2. **Soloist:** When you love to do things on your own and be the star of your show, that's the soloist. They find leadership hard because they don't know how to delegate or accept help. They fear that asking for assistance will expose their incompetence and make them look like they can't handle the weight. In fact, no one has the right to take the shine off them because doing it alone proves exceptionality.

3. **Natural Genius:** They're the know-it-all, so new knowledge for them is hard work. What happened to all their skills and talent? These folks will be least attentive when in a workshop or seminar because their competence, if anything, should come effortlessly and instantaneously. They struggle on the first try, and their self-perception is that they're naturally talented individuals.

4. **Expert:** You believe your knowledge or experience is only a drop in an ocean of water. Year after year, you bag certificates and increase qualifications and still find yourself in the zone where you doubt your legitimacy. It's a case of being an expert by name but not by belief.

5. **The Comparer:** According to Mike Robbins, this individual is caught in a comparison trap with the tendency to be a jealous character who spends more time comparing themselves to others, believing that everyone around them is more competent and accomplished. They feel inadequate and fear being exposed as less capable, so without knowing it, this envy surfaces once they notice someone else doing what they should be doing.

Instead of wishing to be like them, try appreciating what you have.

HOW TO OVERCOME IMPOSTER SYNDROME?

The one thing a victim of impostor syndrome has is talent. They have the skills but need more trust to celebrate their potential. So, how can you overcome your negative thoughts about yourself?

1. **Acknowledge:** Like any other disorder, acknowledgment is the first step to recovery. Accept that you are a victim of impostor syndrome based on all the signs discussed, and then begin the journey of healing by telling yourself it's not unusual and can be corrected. When you admit your wrongdoing, you weaken the chances of repeating the same act twice since you've become aware, present, and hungry for change.

2. **Play down on criticism:** It's good to criticize your work so the best can come out of it. However, in the case of an imposter syndrome mindset, it's safer to go minimal on pinpointing and downgrading your efforts. You might think it's a humbling way to win attention, but you're slowly instilling low self-confidence in yourself. Even if there are hiccups here and there, appraise how well you've performed and prepare more strategically for more significant projects.

3. **Call your impostor syndrome's bluff:** This might sound like pushing yourself to the edge to prove a point. And yes, it is but with a foresight to see yourself disengaging the thought that you don't have what it takes to stand out. Prove everyone—especially yourself—wrong by trusting and taking it all the way.

4. **Listen and learn:** Many people in your circle, probably those you've read about, have been there before. Take a moment to listen to their story and learn from their experiences. No one can help you better than someone who's been there. They know the signs; they'll tell you when to fight hard or pipe low.

5. **Ask for help:** Once you notice it's getting out of hand and your work and position are in jeopardy because of innate negativity, it's time to seek professional support. Let the therapists do their job and help you navigate this challenging phase.

6. **Be mindful:** Choose your words and thoughts carefully as they shape a significant part of your impostor syndrome recovery. As a leader, being positive is a non-negotiable attitude to becoming an achiever and a profiting executor. No matter how bad it all looks, focus on why you want to make the best out of the worst situation.

7. **Take self-care seriously:** Sometimes, the weight on your shoulder strengthens the doubt. You tell yourself, "I'm tired, so

why should I try so hard when it all comes down to nothing?" Instead of all that, aim to take a break in whatever way works for you. Swimming, meditating, taking long walks, getting a sauna treatment, you name it. Always step aside to reboot so your thought level reevaluates things rationally.

8. **Practice collaboration and teamwork:** Once you admit that, yes, you are good, but you don't have all the answers, it will push you to find out who does. And then, you'll appreciate the importance of employees and building a synergized work setting where everyone aims for the success of the other's project. No room for envy, comparison, or judgment, just support, hard work, respect, and team effort.

The strongest weapon impostor syndrome uses to hamper the success of its victim is to kill their self-confidence. You never feel right about anything, and it's the worst place to be when you're a leader. People depend on your optimism and confidence to have a reason to hope, and if that's dashed, then what? Does it mean you'll no longer get the respect and submission of your employees?

If it only takes confidence and determination to make a good leader, then most recognized names today wouldn't make it past the first few months in their positions.

Note that when a leader lacks confidence and has traces of self-doubt, they may sound the same; however, there are some acute differences.

Building confidence involves recognizing and leveraging strengths, setting and achieving goals, seeking feedback, and continuously learning and developing skills. These actions are positive approaches to help individuals develop a sense of competence and self-assurance in their professional abilities.

On the other hand, combating self-doubt focuses on addressing and challenging negative thoughts, beliefs, and insecurities that may undermine confidence. It is about restraining negative self-talk, embracing mistakes and failures as learning opportunities, seeking support from others, and practicing self-care to nurture a positive mindset.

How to Crush Self-Doubt?

The strategies to combat self-doubt and deal with negative thoughts are the same. Try these six tricks:

1. **Challenge negative thoughts:** Your thoughts must constantly be reevaluated whenever you're around people. Once you notice you're about to get into the zone where you practically nurse negative ideas, replace them with positive and realistic ones.

2. **Focus on strengths and accomplishments:** You have records of great success stories; remind yourself of them and all the strengths that have contributed to them. Use these thoughts to boost your confidence and reflect on your capabilities.

3. **View failure as a learning opportunity:** View failure and when you're in doubt as a chance to learn, grow and try again. In one of her lyrics, the late American Singer Aaliyah said, "What if you don't succeed; dust yourself up and try again." Adopt a growth mindset to see setbacks as stepping stones to future success.

4. **Attempt self-compassion:** What recharges you? Is it exercise, relaxation, yoga techniques, or spending time with loved ones? Prioritize it and treat yourself with kindness and understanding during challenging times and moments when you fall below expectations.

5. **Celebrate achievements:** Imagine yourself succeeding and overcoming a back-breaking obstacle; how would you celebrate? Would you take on a bigger challenge to validate your accomplishments, no matter how small? Would you rework your mindset to have better self-belief and motivation? Question your mode of recognizing efforts and be open to good cheer.

6. **Seek feedback and support:** Surround yourself with trusted mentors, colleagues, friends, and professionals to help where necessary. You need people who can provide constructive, open conversations to gain perspective and reassurance that you're in this place of doubt for now, but it's a step toward something amazing.

These tricks, once applied, raise a personality that's slowly beginning to see yourself differently.

BOOST YOUR CONFIDENCE

In leadership, it is important to exude positivity even when the situation looks pretty bad. Gaining that level of respect from subordinates starts with boosting your confidence and making bold decisions. There are several ways to do it, and one thing you must remember is that confidence is about something other than standing tall, speaking professionally, taking a slow and steady stride, and convincing people easily. It's about doing everything possible as a leader to escape and stay safe from that fear of being wrong. It's a horrible place to be enslaved by imposter syndrome. So, start now to boost your confidence by:

1. **Reforming yourself:** Ensure your disposition, attire, and discussions exude high confidence. This is the first trick most people disregard but have proven to be over 70% helpful to job seekers and leaders (Cohn, 2021). When they take a good look at you, there needs to be an aura that will make them assured of your capabilities. It starts from the outside.

2. **Surrounding yourself with positive, beneficial activities:** Everything about your life and desire to grow should be linked to positive actions. Take professional training, join workshops and seminars to empower your skills, and attend conferences where you rub shoulders with positive-minded peer groups and top leadership individuals. These all seem casual, but they significantly affect how you think, act, and react where confidence comes into play.

3. **Challenging your safety net:** You've played it safe for far too long. Aren't you tired of being the nice girl who's too diplomatic sometimes? Go over and beyond to see what comes of it. For instance, maybe you have always dreaded giving presentations to the entire sales and marketing team. You could step outside your comfort zone by volunteering to deliver the next presentation or co-host with a teammate. Usually, you would look for any opportunity to escape that responsibility. It's time to leave the safety net behind, go into the ocean, and see what's out there. You'll either sink or swim, but you'll learn.

4. **Rewriting history:** If you have a background of being the rejected stone who's been ignored, overlooked, underrepresented, and taken for granted, rewrite that story. Don't work into your new position, thinking history will repeat itself. Take a new approach to being positive and forward-thinking. This goes especially for female leaders with doors slammed in their faces. Channel those past experiences into present strengths to stir your course to success.

One of the many ways to encourage confidence in female leaders, especially in the workplace, is to leverage the diversity of thought within a working environment, which we will discuss in detail in the next section.

Stereotypes and gender bias must be addressed to ensure there is only room made for mutual respect and team building. Always recognize that everyone thinks differently, and their differences can help unlock innovation and creativity to match and surpass industry standards.

How to Leverage Diversity in the Workplace?

How can female leadership be fostered to nurture respect, teamwork, and innovation in the workplace without compromising their intentions? I say, by leveraging the diversity of thoughts, you can achieve that in the following ways:

- **Have open dialogues:** The work environment has a serious undertone and a formal setting. So, to keep the mood light and the employees responsive, encourage a safe space where team members feel comfortable expressing their unique perspectives and ideas. Encourage more dialogues where they can speak freely and participate in active listening to ensure that diverse viewpoints are heard and respected.
- **Make inclusion a culture:** The value of inclusion must be emphasized. And so, for female leaders to feel safe and create a more embracing space, diverse perspectives and inclusive culture should be an essential part of work ethics. Recognize and celebrate the contributions of individuals from different backgrounds, experiences, and identities. Encourage collaboration

and teamwork, embracing the power of diversity, and you will see how far the creativity and productivity level will bloom.

- **Perform a mixed-duty delegation:** Form teams with a mix of individuals from various backgrounds, expertise, and ways of thinking to come together and perform different responsibilities. This diversity can lead to richer output, increased creativity, and innovative problem-solving. Consider rotating team members across projects to ensure the cross-pollination of ideas with a mixture of people's strengths and weaknesses to complement each other for personal improvement.

- **Constructive debates and health conflicts:** These should never be seen as a hole in the wall or a source of tension; they should be welcomed as new possibilities and opportunities for growth and improvement. When managed effectively, diverse perspectives can lead to better decision-making and outcomes.

- **Invest in diversity training and education:** Provide training and educational opportunities to raise awareness about unconscious bias, stereotypes, and the benefits of diversity of thought. Equip team members with the knowledge and skills to navigate diverse perspectives, promote inclusivity, and challenge any biases hindering collaboration.

SEGUE

As a leader, setting the record straight so everyone works freely and happily is always a great place to start. Remember, you're also on a path to combat impostor syndrome to stay positive-minded and create the right vibes among the people around you. Let them feel motivated and inspired working around you. Every team is a massive part of the success of a leader and their company, so posterity will speak for you once you employ a leadership style to win and sustain your employees' confidence. You can explore Chapter 6 to understand how great leaders stood the test of time and maintained wealth and recognition.

THE POWERFUL DYNAMICS OF THE FEMALE LEADERSHIP STYLE

A leader takes people where they want to go. A great leader takes people where they don't necessarily want to go but ought to be. — Rosalyn Carter (Fallon, 2023)

W hat makes female leadership different? You might say women show empathy because they have high emotions. But there is more; their emotional intelligence makes them able to apply authenticity to their intentions and attentiveness to the details of human activities. Their leadership is about bringing diverse perspectives to the table, encouraging a collaborative team-building work environment, championing an inclusive playing ground, and working resiliently to see organizational success.

Looking back at the former Prime Minister of New Zealand, Jacinda Ardern, her leadership stood out among the most exceptional with global recognition because of her empathetic approach towards crisis situations and her leadership style, which was diplomatic, inclusive, and full of integrity.

Leadership over the years has witnessed a series of changes. The years of having older generation leadership are slowly fizzling away, giving room to many younger characters; inclusion and diversity are becoming integral to fostering good leadership. People have become specific about the leadership styles and values they seek that will inspire them. Having a style is your way of leaving an indelible mark on how you run things so there can be progressive leadership. To achieve a style that works and is accepted by the majority, there are factors to consider, the first being consistency and predictability.

1. Consistency is about you doing everything that makes your leadership transparent, predictable, and reliable. The perfect way to build a solid foundation where team members are assured that they can trust your integrity and decision-making process because you are all about communication, interpersonal relationships, and problem-solving mechanisms.

2. Nothing beats trust; in today's leadership style, it's a massive requirement if you want your team to stand by you. Can you keep your promises and follow through on commitments? Are the people who depend on you assured of fairness and equity where loyalty is concerned? If it's all yes, rest assured that your team won't only have the psychological safety of knowing they are appreciated and respected, but it would give room for an increased workforce.

3. What's most beneficial is the reputable record you create for yourself. Indira Nooyi, the former CEO of PepsiCo, had a style of leadership that labeled her a visionary because of her ability to see consumer trends way ahead of time. When she launched the "Performance with Purpose,' it was about sustaining growth while looking into social and environmental impacts. She adhered to values, principles, and ethical standards, establishing herself as reliable and trustworthy. There is nothing more profiting than showing credibility and opening doors of opportunities to attract top talent.

4. Consistency leads to improved cooperation and communication, eliminating favoritism and ensuring the team's fairness. Team

members understand the leader's expectations, which enhances teamwork, productivity, and mutual understanding.

From inception, it's plain to see that being a consistent leader is about building a character that provides insurance to your leadership. So, every style has its ups and downs and results therein. Take a look at these 12 different leadership styles and understand their complexities.

1. **The Autocrats:** All that concerns them is that they lead, you follow, and you don't have to like it. Your opinion doesn't count because you're a pawn in a chess board moving at the leader's wimp. Such leaders can think fast on their feet, make quick decision-making, and be efficient in crises. But they'll have more employees walking out the door because they kill creativity and innovation with their autocracy. The work atmosphere will always be low and unexciting.

2. **The Democrats:** Without the voice and commitment of the team, they feel useless and baseless, as what they stand for is collaboration. This is a great and sure way to boost employee engagement with the mission to promote diversity and inclusion. On the lower end, waiting for people to be the deciding panel for your next step can slow down your leadership process, make you appear incompetent enough to make decisions, and sometimes leave you with nothing tangible to work with.

3. **The Laissez-Faires:** They have that "I don't care" attitude where they provide minimal guidance and allow employees to make decisions and work autonomously. Employees enjoy the privilege of freedom and autonomy; however, it lays a poor structure for the environment. Where the system is structureless, there can be a lot of chaos and disorganization.

4. **The Transformers:** Inspiration and motivation is their middle name, as they always aim for exceptional performance and personal growth. They undoubtedly promote personal development and push themselves too hard to see it through. This could lead to burnout, and the dreaded impostor syndrome might worsen if it prolongs.

5. **The Transactionists:** Leadership is like a business deal emphasizing demands, rewards, performance rate, and clear expectations. This can benefit economic development but what about team building and collaborative approaches? These are ignored and sidelined with minimal importance rendering a non-empathetic working environment.

6. **The Servants:** The focus is to serve, protect and support others, putting their needs first. It promotes teamwork, collaboration, and a positive work culture. The sad part is that these leaders often get exploited for their good nature to serve. They get pinned down as weak and sometimes indecisive in a bid to be diplomatic.

7. **The Charismatics:** These are the leaders with a lot of character. They have charm, enthusiasm, and an aura of empowering people. Because of their personality, it's easy to feel motivated and inspired around them. But then, when you take away the personality, it just means there is no substance. Such leaders lose traction pretty quickly, except there is something more about them other than charisma.

8. **The Situationists:** A leadership style that adapts to the individual and situational needs of the team. This can be good but will require lots of assessment, check and recheck for decisions to be made. The process is cumbersome, and long-term development is often overlooked.

9. **The Coaches:** They are focused on guiding and developing individuals to reach their full potential. To ensure the success of any worthy cause you're pursuing, investing time and seeking guidance from a skilled and dedicated coaching leader is essential. With their expertise and professional approach, the purpose and objectives of the cause may be protected. The aim of replicating their skillset is defeated.

10. **The Bureaucrats:** This style emphasizes following rules and procedures strictly. They want a system that works with compliance and consistency as their watchwords. An excellent structure, but it could be more flexible and stiff with room for opinions and innovations.

11. **The Adaptives:** They are open to adjust to any situation and flow with the tide. That's the style of leadership that shows flexibility and openness to change.

12. **The Authentics:** The leaders with this leadership style are genuine, transparent, and true to themselves and their values. They hold strongly to ethical behavior and credibility, mostly making them seem too rigid and inflexible. This resonates as the most outstanding style of leadership to be embraced by all, especially females who seek to lead fearlessly.

AUTHENTIC LEADERSHIP

Though many leadership styles exist, for optimal success, authentic leadership stands out for how it makes individuals establish their true selves and capabilities. In today's society, authenticity sets you apart as someone who doesn't joke with integrity and truth. Gaining people's trust is paramount, and if it takes you losing a few friends and trusted allies along the way, so be it. With such character, authentic leaders can inspire people because they are present, aware, and committed to success. They create an environment where team members feel safe to take risks, share ideas, and collaborate effectively.

Honestly, authentic leadership is essential because of its reputation for building trust and addressing people's aversion to deception and inconsistencies. People naturally have an incline to distrust and suspect others, especially when there are little traces of contradictions here and there. These inconsistencies can distract talented employees from their work, resulting in a negative streak that reduces productivity. However, authentic leadership, characterized by trust, transparency, and support, tackles this issue. By being credible, authentic leaders inspire their team members to excel, collaborate effectively, and achieve shared objectives.

Historical records of authentic leaders like Mary Barra (CEO, General Motors), Malala Yousafzai (Activist), and Michelle Obama (Former First Lady), among others, unveil how you can identify the characteristics of an authentic leader in five traits:

- **Self-awareness:** Authentic leaders understand their values, emotions, strengths, and weaknesses. They've spent years through their personal experiences knowing about themselves and their impact on others. This self-discovery has them actively seek to align their behavior with their core principles so people can appreciate what they stand for.
- **Transparency:** They are open, honest, and transparent in their communication. As much as possible, they ensure information is updated, and transactions are accounted for to avoid hidden agendas and foster an environment of trust within their teams.
- **Truthfulness:** For them, outstanding leadership is about honesty and integrity. Every action must be done with a humble mindset to maintain the right standing by admitting mistakes and sustaining integrity in decision-making.
- **Willing:** A leader who is willing to learn, unlearn, recognize limitations, and acknowledge the contributions of others. That's authentic and humble. When you learn from others, long to hear their feedback, and use it to your advantage, you promote your integrity and empower team members.
- **Empathy and integrity:** They always strive to demonstrate empathy by understanding and valuing the perspectives and emotions of others. They show genuine care and consideration for their team members' well-being while still trying to align with their values and ethical standards. It's a character that's noble and humane at the same time.

The list is endless. It's because authentic leadership is unique and highly embraced by team members. In the hands of an authentic leader, team members feel motivated because these leaders know how to create an environment where individuals feel valued, supported, and inspired.

When 'Ramona,' a 37-year-old media communications graduate, sat down for an interview at a prestigious advertising agency, she felt like a fish out of water. Despite her credentials, her personal struggles, including obesity and low self-esteem, greatly overshadow her potential. She wondered if she could succeed among the elite graduates that filled the company's ranks. Yet, halfway through the interview, a remarkable thing happened.

The CEO saw past 'Ramona's' insecurities and recognized a hidden gem. Ignoring societal bias and conventions, she saw a woman who, despite battling impostor syndrome, held the untapped potential to propel the company forward.

The CEO seized the moment, engaging 'Ramona' in a heartfelt discussion about her worth and value to the company. This wasn't favoritism—it was empathic leadership in action, a potent tool for igniting dormant potential. Authentic leaders excel at this. They empower their team members, foster collaboration, provide constructive feedback, and celebrate accomplishments, steering their teams towards shared objectives. They see beyond perceived limitations and help their people uncover their best selves.

It's why authentic leaders can motivate teams and introduce a method that can swiftly combine with the leadership style of some of the previously mentioned styles for optimal success.

Best Leadership Style Combinations

1. Transformational leaders inspire and motivate their team members by setting high expectations, fostering creativity, and promoting individual growth. So once you combine it with authentic leadership, a powerful blend inspires others to reach their full potential while building trust and authenticity within the organization.
2. Servant leaders prioritize the well-being and development of their team members. They work well with authentic leaders to build a supportive environment where leaders genuinely care about their employees and have a shared sense of purpose.
3. Democratic leaders involve their team members in decision-making, valuing their input and perspectives and seeing ways to rope their ideas into the scheme of things. Connecting this with authentic leadership promotes transparency, open communication, and inclusivity. Here employees feel empowered to contribute ideas and foster a sense of ownership and engagement.
4. Coaches are all about developing the skills and abilities of their team members through mentorship and guidance. Like authentic

leaders, their goal is to provide a support structure and growth-oriented culture for their team members.

All these connections show that authentic leadership is a perfect partner for almost any individual who wants their mode of leadership to resonate differently.

How to Maintain Authenticity?

Any female leader who wants to develop and maintain authenticity for the long term should never forget these eight short quick steps:

1. Reflect on your core values and beliefs.
2. Practice self-awareness and self-reflection.
3. Seek feedback from others.
4. Develop emotional intelligence.
5. Build genuine relationships.
6. Embrace vulnerability and authenticity.
7. Align your actions with your values.
8. Continuously learn and grow as a leader.

Following these steps, you'll leverage a leadership style aiming for success, especially in the workplace, because you've come so far in establishing trust and credibility through consistent transparency. People feel inspired and motivated when you lead passionately with unwavering commitment. Best of all, your open communication and collaborative approach have unlocked your teams' full potential, driving more innovation and increased productivity.

All these have created an authentic female leader whose leadership style demonstrates empathy, support for growth and development, and a positive workplace culture that attracts top talent, enhances employee engagement, and paves the way for long-term success in the organization.

SEGUE

Your leadership style has a significant impact on those around you. It sets the tone, inspires others, and commands respect, regardless of biases.

Always leverage your leadership style to its fullest potential and maintain consistency once you have identified your most effective approach. Doing so will cultivate a growth mindset that aligns with your leadership style, enabling continuous improvement and success. Do you have a growth or fixed mindset? Chapter 7 will educate you better.

CHAPTER 7
THE FEARLESS GROWTH MINDSET

The best thing you can do for the whole world is make the most of yourself. —Wallace Wattles (Hannah, 2020)

Perhaps you didn't know this, but achieving success in life has never been done through a fixed destination. It's fluid and evolves with our changing mindset because our goals never stop expanding even though we have accomplished our initial desires. Maintaining this leadership perspective requires adopting a growth mindset where our intelligence is nurtured and developed based on the boundless capacity to acquire new skills.

Only you have the power to unleash the extraordinary growth mindset within you. But what is this mindset all about?

A growth mindset is an understanding that your abilities and intelligence can be developed and improved through effort, consistent learning, and persevering through tough challenges. To keep yourself upbeat, always recognize that your talents and skills are not fixed traits but can be enhanced with new knowledge and positive influence. According to the Harvard Business Review, a growth mindset challenges the misconceptions that we either have what it takes to grow or we don't, leading to success. Notice that the right attitude, strategies, and support can lead you to grow continually and achieve greater performance and fulfillment in various areas of your life. An American Leadership Coach, Linda Scott, says, "Being an adult and having a growth mindset, you must possess the hunger to learn, fail, make findings, expand, and evolve." (*LinkedIn*, n.d.)

COMMON MYTHS

It means a growth mindset is a process that can be sequential sometimes, which explains why there is a common myth about either having it or not having it. You're either born with the innate desire to grow or appreciate the comfort zone and are too scared to make changes. Although this might sound like a trait of many people, research has shown that everyone can develop a growth mindset with intentional effort and practice. For instance, 'Jenny' worked as a jeweler for a company for over 15 years, and it paid her bills and gave her enough time for her family, which is great. Then one day, it dawns on her that she is made for more and can become her own boss. All it takes is doing research, assessing all the risks and successes involved, and taking the bold step of trying to start as a fearless leader with a potentially growing mindset. This is called emancipating from being okay with the normal to trying something new and promising, which is what a growth mindset is all about.

Another myth is the belief that effort alone can lead to success. While effort is essential, it must be coupled with practical strategies, feedback, and continuous learning to maximize growth. It's why 'Jenny' could pull off and envision her potential as a standalone owner. You need to create room for a mental assessment of what you want and what it will take to get there. That's the start.

There is also the myth that people mistakenly think that a growth mindset dismisses the importance of natural talent or that it guarantees instant success. In reality, a growth mindset values and requires effort and innate abilities because the combination emphasizes the importance of embracing challenges, persisting through setbacks, and seeking opportunities for growth and improvement.

To develop and maintain a growth mindset, it is crucial to acknowledge that growth and learning are lifelong processes. The Harvard Business Review believes you must prioritize confronting and addressing limitations and shortcomings as valuable learning opportunities rather than personal deficiencies. Spending time cultivating self-awareness and seeking feedback from others can help identify areas for growth and improvement. Don't feel too proud or shy to have your ideas and works criticized and evaluated because there is no improvement for hidden work. Constantly challenge yourself and your ideas by stepping out of your comfort zones and taking proactive steps to move forward on continuous development. Once you're at this point, it's the beginning of breaking free from all fixed mindset ideology.

GROWTH VS. FIXED MINDSETS

Observing all the components of a growth mindset presents an apparent contrast to a fixed mindset. While a fixed mindset assumes that our abilities and intelligence are static traits that cannot significantly change, a growth mindset believes in the potential for growth and development. With a growth mindset, individuals understand that their current skills and talents are starting points and that they can expand their abilities through dedication, learning, and effort. If Ben Carson had listened to the voices that criticized his poor learning skills, he wouldn't have become the renowned American neurosurgeon, author, and politician who is celebrated today. That's what a growth mindset can do—it fosters a belief in the power of progress and the capacity for personal transformation.

Critical Devices

But it all begins with some critical devices:

- Don't be ambiguous and scared to experience challenges, setbacks, and self-doubt. It is a shared human experience that needs to happen so you understand there is room for improvement and resilience.
- Aim to use effective strategies, seek support, and believe in your potential for growth.

- Replace limiting beliefs and negative self-talk with positive and affirming statements. Say proudly, "I can learn" and "I can improve."
- Cultivate optimism, curiosity, and a willingness to embrace new opportunities for learning and development.

Above all, let your thinking patterns and beliefs switch into a more daring and adventurous mode where your vision and mission are value-based, and expansions personified.

DEVELOPING A GROWTH MINDSET

No matter how far you go in life, keep developing a growth mindset by:

- **Cultivating a sense of purpose:** Find meaning and direction in your growth journey, keeping your goals and aspirations in mind.
- **Celebrate others, especially your team:** Foster a collaborative and supportive environment by recognizing and celebrating the achievements and growth of your team members.
- **Value growth over speed:** Prioritize continuous improvement rather than focusing solely on immediate results. Embrace the process of development and progress.
- **Take action:** Put your growth mindset into action by consistently taking steps towards your goals, learning new skills, and applying them practically.
- **Welcome constructive criticism:** Welcome feedback and constructive criticism as opportunities for personal growth and development. See them as valuable insights for improvement.
- **Reframe failure:** Change your perspective on failure, viewing it as a steppingstone to learning and growth. Embrace the lessons and insights gained from failures.
- **Engage in reflection and self-thought:** Regularly reflect on your experiences, challenges, and successes to gain deeper insights and adjust for continuous growth.
- **Learn from team mistakes:** Recognize that mistakes happen and view them as learning opportunities. Learn from the mistakes

of others on your team to avoid similar pitfalls and foster collective growth.

- **Embrace the power of "Yet":** Replace limiting beliefs with the understanding that you can develop skills and abilities over time. Shift from "I can't do it" to "I can't do it yet," emphasizing the growth potential.
- **Celebrate growth and progress:** Acknowledge and celebrate your achievements, regardless of their size. Recognize your progress, using it as motivation to continue pushing yourself and striving for excellence.

By striving for excellence, it's not enough to see yourself at the top; you must find the best ways to get up there and maintain a high standard. It comes with its demands, one of which is the act of upskilling.

UPSKILLING

In today's world, upskilling is becoming the in-demand lookout for most employment agencies. Leaders are beginning to see how important it is to up their game, challenging their employees to be more daring in stepping up their own game. This can only mean that upskilling is the future of development and improved performance. Adding more knowledge to what you have because you want to create relevance is the beginning of upskilling. In a survey conducted by LinkedIn in 2020, 94% of employees confirmed they would stay longer with a company that invested in their career development, and 58% of employees said they would be more likely to recommend their organization as a great place to work if they felt supported in their upskilling efforts (*LinkedIn*, n.d.).

Benefits of Upskilling

With the statistics provided above, we can infer that the benefits of upskilling are numerous and continue to grow with time.

- Upskilling programs generate a strong return on investment (ROI) and are often cheaper than addressing workplace problems. With upskilling, the performance grows at its best, leaving room for little to no slips that can cost the company huge debts.

- Providing free training increases employee retention rates and reduces turnover and hiring costs. With more employees willing to take on upskilling learning, it's easier to swing people around job roles rather than bring in new talent. Plus, employees always look for room to grow, so why not give them the best and see them at their best? With Upskilling, employee engagement improves, and their demands for professional development and training opportunities are well satisfied.
- Employee productivity is optimized by improving their understanding and proficiency in relevant technologies. In the age of technology, employees must be carried along, and what better way to do it than to upskill their knowledge and prepare them for the evolving technological era?
- Employees feel an increasing motivation to try and learn new things.
- Upskilling enhances consumer satisfaction by improving the employee experience and enabling them to solve consumer issues better. Their sense of empathy and enthusiasm to meet needs and build better communication comes with passion and professionality.
- Organizations stay competitive by keeping up with industry trends and acquiring new skills to meet the changes in the market. Nothing passes them because they always aim to be way ahead.

That's the idea behind adding more skills to what you have. There is never a case of too much because everything is relevant.

Upskilling vs. Reskilling

There have been several misconceptions about the connections and simi-larities between "Upskilling" and the concept of "Reskilling." Although both aim toward career development and improved job performance, their approaches differ.

In upskilling, you're all about acquiring additional skills and enhancing existing skills to keep up with evolving job requirements and industry trends within a particular field. You want to attain a more profound under-standing or proficiency in specific areas, so you work at expanding exper-tise and staying relevant. While reskilling involves acquiring entirely new skills to transition into a different job or field. It typically occurs when individuals need to shift their career paths due to technological advancements, changes in industry demand, or other factors that make their existing skills obsolete and need an upgrade.

For instance, Sarah, a software developer, recognized the changing demands of the industry. She pursued upskilling to deepen her knowledge of emerging technologies like machine learning. Intrigued by blockchain, she reskilled herself and became a proficient blockchain developer. Sarah's combined efforts in upskilling and reskilling allowed her to navigate the evolving technology landscape and build a rewarding career path. She wasn't scared of the extra demands on her to learn and relearn; instead, she was hungry to try another path to her career. Like Karen Salmansohn, a motivational speaker and author, says, "A successful woman builds a firm foundation with the bricks others have thrown at her." (*Karen Salmansohn Quotes (Author of How to Be Happy, Dammit)*, n.d.)

Upskilling Strategies

As an influential female leader, you should encourage individuals, especially women, to embrace challenges and setbacks as opportunities for growth. By continuously building upon their skills and adapting to new circumstances, they can construct a solid foundation for success, regardless of obstacles.

To achieve this, every leader needs an excellent upskilling strategy to provide a long-lasting skill with 110% ROI traction. These can be:

- Identify skills gaps and target specific areas for improvement. Don't be content with the usual. Always aim to bring something new and fresh to change the status quo.
- Provide ongoing training and development opportunities, such as workshops, webinars, and online courses. As often as possible, every trend in the market should be discussed in roundtables to see how this can be learned and incorporated with best practices maintained.
- Implement mentorship programs and job rotations to offer valuable learning experiences. As a leader, make the job

interesting for employees by switching things up occasionally to avoid making the job monotonous.

- Conduct assessments and evaluations to determine skill needs. Checkmating employees' work delivery and standards will help assess how everyone's deficiency can be restructured and strengthened.
- Integrate upskilling into daily routines, such as dedicating time during lunch breaks for self-study and fostering knowledge-sharing sessions with colleagues for mutual upskilling and learning.
- Utilize online learning platforms like Coursera, Udemy, LinkedIn Learning, and more to encourage employees to access free growth opportunities. Along the way, they can leverage resources and workshops provided by professional associations and organizations. Some of the courses can be (*Leadership Courses: Online Training to Inspire and Lead*, n.d.):

1. "Leadership and Influence" by Dale Carnegie.
2. "Leading with Emotional Intelligence" by Daniel Goleman.
3. "Strategic Leadership and Management" by Stanford University.
4. "Leadership Communication" by Harvard University.
5. "Leading Teams: Inspiring Excellence" by the University of Michigan.
6. "Executive Leadership Development Program" by Wharton School of Business.
7. "Leading for Success: Emotional Intelligence in Leadership" by Case Western Reserve University.
8. "Leadership in 21st Century Organizations" by Copenhagen Business School.
9. "Leadership and Management" by University of California, Irvine.

They are moves that shape the mind for growth, opportunities that shouldn't be taken lightly if, as a leader, you want to be remembered for fearlessness and authenticity. Take note, though, that as good as this gets, there are still pitfalls every leader must avoid while journeying into a growth mindset through upskilling.

PITFALLS

Understand that this is a digital era, and the approach to learning has taken a new dimension. You can either key into it or stay old-fashioned, a common mistake most leaders make. You must rely on something other than formal education or training programs about theories and principles with loads of reading. Half the time, you will lose your audience to confusion and indifference. You must consider the practical application and balance theoretical knowledge and hands-on experience.

Another pitfall is providing available skills instead of what is necessary. As a leader who fully understands their company, you must know what is relevant and required to make your employees stand out. Irrelevancies will only keep employees behind the competition when new opportunities arise. So, continuously reassess skills because industries evolve rapidly; you must envision what will be valuable.

It is essential to conduct a comprehensive self-assessment of your workforce to avoid a one-size-fits-all approach. Recognize that while some employees have the potential to learn and improve their skills, others thrive when immersed in hands-on tasks. As a collaborative leader, these evaluations are always at your fingertips to understand that different individuals may have unique learning preferences. It is in your place to provide diverse learning opportunities that can cater to these various styles and needs so you can create a variety of learning and a hunger for upskilling. This, in turn, leads to enhanced job retention and high recommendation to any organization.

Strategies to Avoid Pitfalls

Achieving upskilling requires smart strategies applied at the slightest opportunity while avoiding pitfalls. Learning doesn't have to feel demanding or tiresome because there are ways to make it convenient, engaging, and exciting simultaneously.

- **Break-time sessions with experts:** Organize sessions during lunch breaks where outside specialists share their knowledge on specific subjects. Encourage participation and create a supportive environment for continuous learning.

- **Virtual learning and training:** Utilizing technology with online software is a great way to provide employees with the flexibility to train remotely at their convenience. Allocate necessary resources and promote participation to ensure successful implementation.
- **Mentoring by experienced employees:** Tap into the expertise of internal mentors to provide on-the-job training and guidance. Foster a learning culture and recognize achievements to encourage both mentors and mentees.
- **Microlearning sessions:** Offer short, focused training sessions, such as videos followed by exercises and quizzes, that can be completed in minutes. Provide easily accessible materials and track progress to ensure effective learning outcomes.
- **Develop a comprehensive plan:** Identify skills gaps and create a tailored upskilling plan. Allocate resources, provide guidance, and track progress to achieve desired outcomes.
- **Foster a learning culture and encourage participation:** Promote the benefits of upskilling, actively engage employees in opportunities, and create an environment that values continuous learning.
- **Provide support, guidance, and recognition:** Offer necessary support and advice to employees throughout their upskilling journey. Recognize and reward achievements to motivate and reinforce the importance of ongoing development.

SEGUE

You see it, too, don't you?

Being hungry for growth can take you to places you never thought possible. That's the power of having the right mindset. So, embrace upskilling, and keep striving for more success. It's an endless journey that fuels your development and makes you the kind of leader every employee yearns to work side by side with. As we move forward, let's explore the next chapter, where you will discover what drives you for success.

CHAPTER 8

FIND YOUR "WHY" AND LEAD WITH PURPOSE

Hard work is painful when life is devoid of purpose. But when you live for something greater than yourself and the gratification of your ego, hard work becomes a labor of love. —Steve Pavlina (Nemeth, 2020)

If you haven't understood that your being in this life is not by accident but intentional, then you don't know how valuable you are. The first rule to living a fulfilled and purposeful life is knowing you were born to make a difference to yourself and the people around you. Once you're thinking this way, you create room to pursue success and see how worthwhile it is to find yourself and use your superpower to inspire others.

In trying to find purpose, individuals always have questions lined up:

- Why am I different?
- Why is it vital for me to learn this or that?
- Why do I need to do this and that?
- Why does it matter to them or me?

These questions are expected and relevant for anyone seeking to grow, succeed and create visionary ideas to inspire and motivate more people. Women always go through this phase at some point in their lives. So many questions about life pop up in their head, and it feels like an enormous weight is on their shoulders because they need answers and fast. A lot depends on how the answers they receive impact their lives and those who look up to them. The famous writer/author Maya Angelou said, "Each time a woman stands up for herself, without knowing it possibly, or even claiming it, she stands up for all women." (Top 25 Quotes By Maya Angelou *TOP 25 (of 1010) | A-Z Quotes*, n.d.)

In working to create relevance for women's place in leadership, especially in the workplace, you are awakening more women to understand their purpose, find themselves, and align their needs to establish the best version of themselves. This brings us back to the question of "why". How does your "why" matter in helping you succeed and enabling your team to become driven? Among many things, the answer can be found in Maslow's Hierarchy of Needs.

MASLOW'S HIERARCHY OF NEEDS

It's a theory that proposes that every individual has a flow of needs to be met before they can acknowledge that they are living their best life. This flow illuminates the path to passion, motivation, and inspiration that every leader should possess to transfer this self-actualization to their employees for maximum satisfaction equally.

It starts with how you arrive at meeting your needs systematically, so you reach your fullest potential and lead a truly fulfilling life.

Maslow's Pyramid of needs is often called a psychological framework for understanding individual needs and their interplay. Once done, you can gain valuable insights into what drives human behavior and what it takes to achieve self-actualization. In leadership, you can hold the four aces since you'll fully grasp what can make your employees tick and commit to job success.

Simply put, Maslow aligns five stages of fulfilling life needs so everyone gets to understand at what stage they are at to get to the apex point of their life. From the basic physiological needs required for survival, such as food, water, and shelter, to the higher-level needs of love and belonging, self-esteem, and self-actualization, the pyramid displays the human journey toward personal growth.

Suppose you're interested in an existence that involves self-improvement. In that case, this is definitely the model to follow, and it's what many great female leaders have followed to arrive at the pinnacle of their careers.

Recall the story of Malala Yousafzai, a courageous advocate for girls' education, who, despite facing adversity in Pakistan, recognized the importance of fulfilling basic physiological needs, such as safety, education (which was greatly frowned upon for women), and healthcare. She prioritized her safety while continuing to speak out, defying the oppressive Taliban regime and striving for a safer future for girls because she believed there was more for girls than living in relegation. With the loving support of her family and a global network she connected to for her fight, Malala found a sense of belonging, empowering her to persist in her mission and motivating more girls to rise up for their rights. While receiving international recognition and awards, Malala remained humble, using her platform to amplify marginalized voices and fight for equality. Her advocacy has stirred many awakenings in the Middle East, Asia, and Africa. Through her unwavering dedication, Malala achieved self-actualization, establishing the Malala Fund, and advocating for girls' education worldwide. Malala's story unveils a perfect example of how a female leader who accomplishes life needs can drive more leaders and women to overcome obstacles, inspire change, and make a lasting impact.

Maslow's Hierarchy of Needs showcases that specific prerequisites, such as freedom of speech and living in a just society, can greatly help the natural progression of life. Learning and understanding the world around us is essential, serving practical and innate purposes. Although needs are presented in a hierarchy, they are not strictly linear, and individuals often have partially met needs. Furthermore, one behavior can satisfy multiple needs simultaneously. Maslow's insights remind us that our journey through the hierarchy is complex and interconnected, shaping our pursuit of fulfillment and self-actualization.

What Are "Needs"?

With the theory comes a definition of the needs in every individual's desired path for an accomplished life. We can divide our needs into two parts: deficiency and growth needs.

Deficiency Needs

Deficiency needs are the lower level that arises when you feel deprived or lacking in something of a necessity. Call them the essentials of survival and well-being that prompt individuals to seek satisfaction. They include the first four levels of the hierarchy:

- **Physiological needs:** These are the basic biological needs for survival, such as food, water, shelter, sleep, and physical well-being —everything you need to feel comfortable and stress-free, so you don't get overwhelming worries.
- **Safety and security needs:** It's all about having a secure and stable environment free from physical or psychological harm. They include personal safety, financial stability, job security, health, and protection from dangers like harassment, assault, or even disasters.
- **Love and belonging needs:** Everyone needs to network and connect. Your ability to gain acceptance and have meaningful relationships will meet the need to be loved, form friendships, achieve intimacy, belong to a community or group, and have positive interpersonal relationships.
- **Esteem needs:** These needs encompass the desire for self-esteem and recognition from others. They involve feelings of self-worth, confidence, achievement, respect from others, and the need for recognition or status. Deficiency needs might be on the lower level, but they motivate individuals to strive to meet up, knowing that the absence creates a sense of dissatisfaction. However, once met, individuals can progress to higher-level needs, known as growth or being needs.

Growth Needs

These are the higher-level needs in Maslow's Pyramid. Unlike deficiency needs, which arise from deprivation, growth needs to emerge from a desire for personal development and realizing one's potential. If you want to stand out and impact, these needs demand a focus on self-actualization and pursuing meaning and purpose in life. You can pinpoint them as:

- **Cognitive needs:** The desire for knowledge, understanding, and intellectual growth. It's a never-ending quest to acquire all aspects of learning and keeps individuals seeking to expand their intelligence, engage in academic pursuits, and explore new ideas and concepts.
- **Aesthetic needs:** Aesthetic needs involve appreciating beauty, art, and creativity. Your aesthetic pleasure is put to work. What is your love for modern art, music, nature, or other forms of creative expression? These are the desires that are sort-after.
- **Self-actualization:** The highest level of the hierarchy represents the need for personal growth, fulfillment, and realizing one's full potential. Transcendence, as some studies call it, is the high point of your life where you're all about growth and authenticity, and your journey toward self-actualization and personal growth becomes uniquely different from others based on how you want self-actualization to reflect in your story.

EXPANDED THEORY OF MASLOW'S HIERARCHY OF NEEDS

The great thing about Maslow's Pyramid is its timelessness. Through generations, it remains the most realistic attempt to comprehend human needs. Although, time has shown that with the evolution of human behavior, man has become hungry for more and dissatisfied with the usual. It's why in the 1970s, researchers embarked on a study to see how they could develop an Expanded Theory of Maslow's Hierarchy of Needs.

It's why the five motivational levels, which have always been known as Maslow's Pyramid, conceptualized in 1943, had three more needs added, as seen above. As many questioned the importance of these additions to what has been known and accepted overtime as to affected individuals and leadership goals, the key takeaway in recognizing these evolving needs was:

- The expanded theory recognizes that particular prerequisites, such as freedom of speech and living in a just society, facilitate needs. Once these external factors are met, it creates an enabling environment for individuals.
- The importance of learning and understanding the world around us is emphasized. The knowledge expands to gain insights about our environment and how you can contribute to meeting specific needs and fulfilling an inherent desire.
- Needs go beyond being hierarchical or linear because individuals often have partially met needs at any given time. Also, their progress through the hierarchy may vary as needs can become more complex and dynamic.
- Needs are more interconnected within the hierarchy than ever before. A behavior or action can address multiple needs simultaneously, bringing about a holistic accomplishment through integrated experiences.

SELF-ACTUALIZATION

In all the dialogues on needs discussed over the years, self-actualization is the most paramount used by individuals and leaders, especially to motivate themselves and inspire others with the truth. They can live their best and most purposeful life if they key into what they define as needful.

For instance, in the workplace, when you refer to self-actualized leaders, it's those who have attained a state where their employees know and recognize that they are authentic, they rose through the ladder by accepting their potential, and they let failures become their stepping stones. And now, these leaders are paying it forward by inspiring more people to go on the same journey causing a positive ripple effect throughout the organization. An effect that's empowering enough to recreate employees that go above and beyond to see projects through confidently.

As an individual threading the job market in search of the perfect place to grow and evolve, how can you identify these leaders? What are the characteristics of a self-actualized individual who can lead you to your golden room? The seven important attributes of these leaders are:

1. **Self-awareness:** They understand their strengths, weaknesses, values, and passions. So no one can deceive them into feeling little or having low self-esteem because they've grown above that level.
2. **Defined purpose:** These individuals are purpose-driven. They have a clear focus on what they want, and it guides their actions and decisions. They aren't random but prepared for every step they want to take as they progress.
3. **Continuous learning:** Any chance for growth is always noticed. New knowledge for them is like buying the latest model of a Ferrari. It's fulfilling, so they go for professional development opportunities, attend seminars, workshops, and conferences, and expand their knowledge and skills.
4. **Authenticity:** One thing you can't take away from them is their genuineness, transparency, and staying true to their values. It gives room for those unique personalities and perspectives to shine through.
5. **Meaningful connections:** They are big on interpersonal relationships and connections by engaging in networking, mentorship, and collaboration opportunities.
6. **Taking risks:** They always desire to step outside their comfort zones and seek new responsibilities. In fact, they want to try as many new things as possible, so there is always the willingness to take calculated risks.
7. **Inspire and empower others:** Success for them alone is only possible if they can support the growth and development of team members and provide mentorship, coaching, and recognition. Only then can they proudly say that it was all worth it.

These are the most unignorable characteristics of anyone who truly believes in self-actualization and wants to be authentic in the workplace. But, understand that character goes beyond this.

Benefits of Self-Actualization

Self-actualization benefits everyone because once you arrive at this point in your life, you feel satisfied and joyful about everything, even if things look difficult. You radiate a positive energy that's infectious for the organization or the community you are part of. You awaken this person inside who is all about the greater good and contributing to societal growth. So, somehow, it's a character that goes beyond you to the person next to you, and before you know it, it covers the whole environment.

When it comes to the purpose of the workplace and leadership, self-actualization comes with many benefits:

- **Enhanced job satisfaction:** When individuals align their work with their personal values, passions, and purpose, they experience a deeper level of job satisfaction because everything is coming together. They find meaning and happiness in their roles, which translates into increased enthusiasm, motivation, and engagement in their work.
- **Increased performance:** Self-actualized individuals are driven, fueling their dedication and commitment to achieving their goals. This heightened motivation and focus lead to improved productivity and performance in the workplace. Their records are outstanding, and more times, they can go above and beyond, taking the initiative and delivering high-quality results.
- **Authentic and inspirational leadership:** It brings about an authenticity that inspires others through actions. By leading purposefully and passionately, they create a positive work culture that encourages and empowers their team members to reach their full potential. They become role models and sources of inspiration, fostering a sense of trust, loyalty, and collaboration within the team.
- **Improved problem-solving:** More employees who self-actualize start to possess a strong sense of self-awareness, which enables them to make more informed decisions and solve problems effectively. They deeply understand their own values, strengths, and limitations, allowing them to approach challenges

with clarity and resilience. This leads to better decision-making and the ability to navigate complex situations confidently.

- **Positive impact:** When leaders prioritize their self-fulfillment and inspire others to do the same, it creates a work environment that values personal growth, purpose-driven work, and authenticity. It also fosters collaboration, trust, and mutual support among team members. This, in turn, enhances teamwork, communication, and overall team performance.

It shows how self-actualization unlocks true potential and numerous benefits in the workplace. The joy of positively contributing to a thriving organizational culture is established. Somehow every individual, from leader to employee, starts to live each day to its fullest, knowing they are all making meaningful impacts in different ways and creating fulfilling professional experiences.

But, to get to that place where you self-actualize means there is a "why" in the life goal. Why should this path be important to you as a leader, and why should you find yourself to achieve that purposeful life?

To answer these questions, you must find your core values. The best way to find these core values is by asking yourself—what makes you exceptional when you put yourself to the test? Is it self-actualization? You will see that what's important to you isn't the same for someone else. However, with these steps, you can acquire self-actualization easily:

1. Engage in introspection and self-reflection.
2. Explore what truly makes you happy and gives you a sense of purpose.
3. Understand your values, strengths, and aspirations.
4. Uncover your unique purpose and meaning as a leader.
5. Lead in a purpose-driven way.
6. Ignite a sense of fulfillment in your leadership journey.
7. Inspire others through your purpose and actions.

You will align your leadership journey with what truly matters to you, fostering a sense of self-actualization and purpose.

Importance of Vision

At this point, when you feel rested and invested in your success, it's normal to question if it's wise to share your purpose or vision. Sharing your purpose as a leader can profoundly impact your team. While it's not necessary to explicitly share every detail, expressing your vision and aligning it with the organization's goals can inspire and motivate others. It can even create new visions to evolve the organization for another level of growth. As more people hear and understand the idea behind the vision, they can contribute to coming up with a fresh perspective. This is as much a plus for you as a leader as it is for your employees. Recognize that leaders who communicate their purpose authentically create a sense of purpose within their teams, fostering a collective commitment towards a common goal.

Once you have identified your purpose and have people channeling their energy in the same lane as yours for optimum purpose, the next step is to implement it. Those practical steps for your daily actions with your vision come with you constantly asking yourself, "What can I do today to live my purpose?" It's simple. Take intentional steps towards your goals by creating a meaningful impact and inspiring others to do the same. It's just what we've been saying, and it doesn't change because that's how you empower yourself and others to lead authentically and passionately.

Now don't think this journey is a walk in the park; in aiming toward self-actualization, it's just as important to address and dispel common myths hindering progress. Debunk misunderstandings about purpose, such as the belief that purpose must be grandiose or solely focused on personal success. Understanding and challenging these myths allows you to embrace your unique purpose and lead in a way that aligns with your authentic self.

Once you've arrived at this stage, congratulations! You are all set to inspire others by becoming the mentor they need to set sail toward their goals.

MENTORSHIP

Mentorship is a powerful tool for personal and professional growth. It offers guidance, support, and the opportunity to learn from someone with experience in your desired field. Research has shown that mentoring works, as it helps individuals develop new skills and reach their goals more effectively. If you're interested in becoming a mentor, it's essential to understand your responsibilities. A great mentor sets goals with their mentees, provides constructive feedback that pushes their mentees to the next level, and challenges them to go ahead of set boundaries. Remember, being a mentor isn't about gatekeeping knowledge; it's about empowering others to succeed in the future using your years of experience.

To get started, try various mentoring activities such as icebreaker exercises (a game of conversation and cool down for people to get acquainted relaxingly), skill-sharing, and inspiring your colleagues and team members.

Advancing women in leadership is crucial for fostering gender equality and creating diverse and inclusive workplaces. Recruiting more women is essential if you want to promote women in leadership roles. Seek out qualified female candidates and ensure the hiring process is fair and unbiased. Additionally, as you provide sufficient training and mentorship opportunities to support their professional development and address any challenges they may face, never forget those with growing skills who need that push away from self-doubt to self-awareness; they are just as important and hungry for growth, and should be carried along. Creating a woman-friendly culture is the future of outstanding leadership because it encourages work-life balance, offers flexible arrangements that won't seem overwhelming, and promotes an inclusive environment that values and respects women's contributions.

Finally, consider advocating for policy changes that promote gender equality, such as implementing supportive policies for maternity leave and childcare, and using digital workplaces to facilitate work-life integration.

SEGUE

By taking these steps, we can inspire and empower women to thrive in leadership positions. Women need this validation to help them come to terms with their chosen career path, the business dreams they want to pursue, or the promotion they hold dear. Once all these come together, it's clear that they've come to their fearless place of branding their legacy. A chapter of their life that will make all the difference.

CHAPTER 9

BE FEARLESS AND
BRAND YOUR LEGACY

Legacy is not what I did for myself. It's what I'm doing for the next generation. —Vitor Belfort (*Legacy Quotes*, n.d.)

When the word "legacy" comes up, many people think it's about wealth, empires, and being a mogul with billboards with your name on them so people acknowledge the generational footprints created through one person's ingenious ideas. It's not a lie, but there is so much more. Ruth Bader Ginsburg, a famous American lawyer, jurist, and Supreme Court associate justice, says it's about "Fight for the things that you care about, but do it in a way that will lead others to join you." (*Ruth Bader Ginsburg Tells Young Women: "Fight for the Things You Care About" | Radcliffe Institute for Advanced Study at Harvard University*, n.d.)

It's that urge to make a difference by making others see things from your perspective, and then they're convinced to join you in standing out for the present and future. You might not know it, but slowly, you're building something profound. It's like a woman who gives birth to a child, believe it or not, a child is a legacy of the name they represent. When you impact meaning and purpose into them, they leave an indelible mark that will uphold their family name for decades. It's the same with a female leader who aims to lead fearlessly.

She doesn't want it so she can prove a point that women need to have equal space to lead and grow like every other male; she needs it to lay a foundation for her growth and the future of young girls and women that will be exceptional for the caliber of leadership the world requires today; one of selflessness and success.

LEAVE A LEGACY!

As a female leader, caring about leaving a legacy is essential for several reasons:

- When you leave a legacy, you inspire other women to follow your lead and drive meaningful change in the professional world. Your accomplishments and your impact serve as a source of inspiration, empowering other women to break barriers and achieve their own success. Call yourself the trailblazer who contributes to shifting the narrative and challenging traditional gender roles. That's who you become and what people see when they look at you.
- Leaving a legacy allows you to change the status quo. It demonstrates your capabilities and achievements and how they have defied stereotypes and paved the way for a more inclusive and equal society. In a study from Pew Society, statistics showed that the gender pay gap in the United States had seen minimal improvement over the past two decades, with women typically earning 82% of every dollar earned by men in 2022, similar to the 80% they earned in 2002. This slow progress contrasts sharply with the significant advancement witnessed in the preceding two decades when women earned only 65% of each dollar earned by men in 1982. It proves that now more than ever, the world needs that female influence and presence to create opportunities for future generations of women. It will help to reduce gender pay gaps and provide a platform for diverse voices to be heard. *(Pew Research Center Finds Gender Pay Gap Has Barely Budged in Past 20 Years, 2023)*

- Moreover, as a female leader, you become a role model and mentor to young girls, show them what is possible, and encourage them to dream big. Your actions and accomplishments convey that women can excel in leadership positions and significantly impact their chosen fields, and that's what the younger generation wants to see. They need to believe that everything is possible with more commitment and drive. You build a more equitable and diverse future by nurturing the next generation of female leaders.
- With a legacy-minded drive, workplaces would be less toxic. Who needs a space filled with back-biting and all sorts of sneaky attitudes? It's demoralizing; it's why your leadership style and values can inspire a positive work culture, fostering collaboration, respect, and inclusivity. There is no drag for superiority based on class, color, or sex but an environment centered on supporting all individuals and contributing to the well-being and success of team members.

Best of all, you become a voice for the voiceless, using your platform to speak out against inequality, discrimination, and social issues, addressing these challenges from the standpoint of someone who's been there and now wants to advocate for change and an inclusive society.

In fact, you'll be pushing towards being the iconic woman they've been waiting for to take them to the next level—someone who has been preparing for a moment like this for years.

BE AN ICONIC FEMALE LEADER!

Now, you must be wondering—how do you become an Iconic Female Leader, Marguerite? I have answers for you:

- By using all the weapons in self-empowering books, especially this one—to transform herself from a girl who accepted the usual to a woman who challenges the unusual so there can be harmonious living.
- By self-assessment and improvement aimed at personal growth, and continuously striving to improve your skills, knowledge, and leadership abilities. Being a leader means investing in self-

development programs, seeking mentorship, and embracing lifelong learning.

- By dreaming big and setting ambitious goals that go beyond societal limitations. No one has the right to tell you that, as a woman, this is as far as you can go or that this is the industry for men; there is little space for women here. Believe in your potential to significantly impact and challenge the status quo. Be fearless in pursuing your aspirations and breaking barriers.
- By developing your skills and expertise so you become indispensable in your field. You already know how it's easy to be put in the background once your ideas no longer seem productive, so continuously enhance your knowledge, acquire new competencies, and stay ahead of emerging trends. Be adaptable, resilient, and willing to embrace change. Position yourself as a valuable asset in your organization or industry, one they can hardly decide without consulting.
- By being bold and confident in what you believe in. Be the advocate for equality, inclusivity, positive change, and the woman who champions the underrepresented. You'll find yourself addressing critical issues that impact women in the workplace.
- By supporting and uplifting others who speak up, creating a culture of inclusivity and empowerment. Foster an environment where everyone feels heard and valued as they raise significant concerns and work collaboratively to drive meaningful change.
- By collaborating and connecting with like-minded individuals and women who share your vision and values. There is so much benefit in forming alliances, joining networks, and participating in professional communities to amplify your impact. You'll find engaging in partnerships and collaborations that promote diversity, innovation, and collective progress easy.
- By cultivating a strong social media presence to amplify your message, connecting with a broader audience, and inspiring others is paramount, especially in this age of technology. Use various platforms to share your experiences, insights, and achievements. Leveraging social media for empowerment, mentorship, and networking is the best way to reach a wider audience of like minds and women who need upliftment.

- By setting high accountability standards for yourself, leading by example, and maintaining integrity. Demonstrate professionalism, ethical behavior, and a strong work ethic where you don't joke with figures and auditing, as it sets a pace for higher expectations and closes all gaps. Strive for excellence and ensure that your actions align with your values. Inspire others through your commitment to personal and professional integrity.
- By cultivating self-awareness to recognize biases and promote fairness and equality. Challenge your assumptions, educate yourself about diversity and inclusion, and actively work to eliminate unconscious biases. Create an environment where everyone feels valued and respected, regardless of gender or background.
- By fostering diversity in the workplace by actively seeking out and hiring talent from diverse backgrounds. Stop paying attention to who comes from where and start promoting equal gender ratios in leadership positions and advocate for inclusive policies and practices. As long as there is productivity and forward-thinking minds, every woman must embrace the power of diverse perspectives, experiences, and ideas to drive innovation and success.

Visualize yourself achieving all the above goals—Now, you're no longer that one voice trying to create relevance; you've built a network for yourself. By being the iconic leader, you used all the tentacles available, from self-improvement to expert support to sharing knowledge. You've gone around, and it's time to let your brand stand through all the networks you've created over time. Building a solid personal brand and making your mark in your industry heavily relies on effective networking. It's about leveraging connections to establish your reputation and amplify your value. Like everything else that needs building, there are strategies you have to adapt to make it achievable and sustainable.

Sustainable Iconic Leadership

1. **Envision your networking goals (The VALUED Model):** What are your networking objectives? You must be clear about this, and then you can visualize the desired outcomes. Understand

your value and how networking can enhance it into becoming more than just a brand but a demand.

2. **Be accepting of various leadership networks:** Explore a range of formal and informal leadership networks that go well with your professional aspirations. These networks offer valuable learning opportunities, mentorship, and potential collaborations. There can be many schools of thought in leadership, so when you find what fits with yours, learn how they made it work and use it.

3. **Ignore networking myths:** Make sure to avoid getting swayed by common misconceptions. They won't only discourage you but leave you, always making excuses. Imagine a myth that says networking is only for extroverts! How can that be possible? Recognize that networking is a skill anyone can develop, regardless of personality type. You can go all the way once you know and hold on to this.

4. **Comprehend the networking structure:** Take the time to grasp the networking structure and how relationships are built and nurtured. Cultivate diverse connections, including peers, mentors, and sponsors, across various industries and backgrounds so you can apply a more grounded networking mode. According to the Harvard Review Issue of 2022, achieving a holistic networking approach is about addressing the operational, personal, and strategic angle of leadership structure; otherwise, there will be an imbalance in service delivery. As you pay attention to the organization's affairs (operational), carry yourself along in development (personal), and ensure you're up-to-date on the latest and the most remarkable innovations. (Arscott, 2022)

5. **Network in terms of resources:** Go beyond simply connecting with people and consider networking in terms of valuable resources. Identify what you need to succeed and seek out individuals who can provide knowledge, expertise, opportunities, or support. This requires your intuitive behavior in singling out quality over quantity. Remember, you're out to be a leader seeking to network productively, so no stone can be left unturned to retrieve the best results.

6. **Share your resources:** It's all about give and take. Be generous in sharing your resources, insights, and experiences by sustaining a

collaborative mindset. Contribute to the success of your network by offering assistance and support.

7. **Stay authentic:** It's crucial to adapt your communication style to the situation but remain true to yourself. No need to throw away what you represent because you feel the circumstances outweigh your principles. No need to swing off course; only practice active listening, display genuine interest in others, and foster relationships based on trust and respect. As you give, also be humble to receive when given because it shows ethical behavior.

8. **Utilize power thoughtfully:** If you have influence or power within your network, exercise it thoughtfully and responsibly. Don't get drunk with authority; instead, focus on your impact on others and use your position to empower and uplift those around you rather than solely for personal gain or a show-off.

9. **Communicate effectively:** Enhance your communication skills to convey your ideas clearly, actively listen to others, and tailor your message to resonate with different individuals. Choose your words wisely, so it doesn't pass the wrong intentions, and be mindful of how your communication can impact relationships.

10. **Negotiate with skill:** Whether discussing opportunities, collaborations, or career advancements. Hone your negotiation skills, advocate for yourself, assert your value, and maintain a collaborative and respectful approach so others' ideas are shown to be just as relevant and impactful as yours. Never give room for bickering because your employees see in you the leader who believes in equity.

11. **Build, maintain, leverage, and transition relationships:** Networking is an ongoing investment in building relationships, nurturing them through regular communication and support, leveraging them to achieve your goals, and being adaptable in transitioning them.

By implementing these strategies, you can develop an authentic and empowering networking approach that will help you cultivate a solid professional network, establish your brand, and unlock new opportunities and collaborations for yourself!

CULTIVATE A NETWORK!

Below are the top five perfect places for you to cultivate networks:

1. **Professional Associations and Industry Events:** For instance, a female leader in the tech industry could attend conferences like the Grace Hopper Celebration, an event dedicated to women in computing. By participating in industry-specific gatherings, she can connect with fellow professionals, attend informative sessions, and build relationships with individuals who share her interests and goals.
2. **Women's Leadership Organizations:** Joining organizations such as the National Association of Women Business Owners (NAWBO) or Women in Technology International (WITI). They provide access to networking events explicitly tailored to empower women in leadership. These events often feature keynote speakers, panel discussions, and workshops on professional development and networking opportunities.
3. **Online Networking Platforms:** LinkedIn, World Pulse, Hub Dot, and Ellevate Network offer virtual spaces for professional women to connect and engage with each other. For instance, a potential female leader can join industry-specific LinkedIn groups, participate in discussions, and connect with professionals with common career interests. These online platforms enable networking opportunities regardless of geographical constraints.
4. **Business Incubators and Accelerators:** Women entrepreneurs can leverage programs like Women's Startup Lab or Female Founders Alliance. These organizations provide access to mentorship and resources and facilitate networking events where aspiring female leaders can connect with successful entrepreneurs, investors, and industry experts who can provide guidance and support.
5. **Diversity and Inclusion Initiatives:** Women can participate in events like the Women in Leadership Summit or The Women's Chapter to network with professionals from diverse backgrounds and industries. These initiatives strengthen connections among women leaders, encourage collaboration, and create spaces for

sharing experiences and best practices in promoting diversity and inclusion.

By actively engaging in these networking opportunities, potential female leaders can broaden their professional networks, gain exposure to new ideas, find mentors and sponsors, and increase their visibility within their industry. You can embark on a remarkable journey to leave a lasting impact on the workplace and society.

SEGUE

By actively networking and building meaningful connections in professional associations, you can position yourself to imprint memories and reshape perceptions of women in leadership roles. Your success will become an inspiration, empowering other women to pursue their own paths to greatness. As you gather your skills, embrace continuous learning, and fearlessly put your plans into action, you become a catalyst for change, leaving imprints deep enough to transform history. Now is the time to step forward and create a legacy that will be remembered for generations.

FUELING THE FUTURE OF LEADERSHIP

Now that you have the insights and tools needed to become a fearless leader, it's time to share your newfound knowledge and guide others to where they can find the same powerful resources.

By leaving your honest opinion of this book on Amazon, you'll direct other aspiring leaders to the guidance they seek and help perpetuate the passion for transformative leadership.

Thank you for your assistance. The art of leadership thrives when we pass on our knowledge—you are playing a vital role in helping me continue this important work.

Your feedback not only supports our community of leaders but also encourages others to embark on their journey of fearless leadership. Your voice matters, and your review can light the way for others to follow.

Thank you once again for being an essential part of this movement. Together, we are keeping the spirit of leadership alive and vibrant.

It's simple to leave a review on Amazon: Visit the book's Amazon 'Write a customer review' page by scanning the code below.

Your support is extremely important to me. Great things can happen from a small gesture!

Leaving a fair and honest review on Amazon would enable other women to know about this book giving them the tools and strategies needed for their leadership journey.

CONCLUSION

As we reach the conclusion of this book, it is clear that fearlessness and confidence are driven by tapping into our authentic selves and embracing our strengths and weaknesses. As a female leader, you will learn that pretending to be someone else is futile, as true success and growth come from aligning our actions with our genuine selves. The notion of "faking it until making it" has been debunked, for it hinders our personal and professional development.

Leave all the worries about gender inequality and doubts that may hinder your path to becoming an iconic and fearless female leader. Believe in yourself, for you have the power to achieve greatness. Hold firmly and strongly to the valuable lessons you have learned throughout this journey and embody your leadership with authenticity, inspiration, and lasting impact. Trust in your abilities and forge ahead with unwavering confidence. Yes, you can, and you will make a difference. The doubt must fade away as you step into your true leadership potential.

In this journey, you have discovered **Nine Unforgettable Strategies** to stay ahead in becoming a fearless female leader:

1. The importance of maintaining authenticity while acquiring soft and hard skills to excel as leaders.

2. You've witnessed the power of finding your voice and ears and mastering effective communication to establish mutual respect, understanding, and collaboration with your colleagues.

3. Risk-taking and learning from failure are two things you can identify as instrumental to any fearless leadership journey, debunking the misconception that female executives take fewer risks.

4. There has been inspiration from the teamwork displayed in the construction of the pyramids, recognizing the value of collaboration and mutual respect and inspiring others to work together towards a shared goal.

5. As leaders, we have explored various leadership styles and recognized the importance of knowing your style, remaining consistent, and inspiring others through your fearless leadership.

6. Your mindset plays a crucial role in shaping your perception of success, as it constantly evolves along with your goals.

7. Adopting a growth mindset ensures you stay on track with an ever-expanding vision for your leadership journey.

8. Moreover, you now understand the significance of finding meaning in your work and valuing what you do for yourself and those around you, inspiring them to strive for excellence.

9. Finally, you explored the concept of workplace legacies, understanding that true success lies in achieving your personal goals and leaving a positive and lasting impact on the business world. Engraving a legacy requires humility, grace, and a genuine desire to inspire others, ensuring that your contributions transcend individual achievements.

When you think about successful fearless female leaders, think about Sheryl Sandberg, Facebook's Chief Operating Officer (COO). She has consistently practiced authenticity, empowering others, effective communication, taking risks, and leaving a lasting legacy. Sandberg is known for her influential book *Lean In*, where she encourages women to pursue their ambitions, challenge gender biases, and lean into leadership roles. Through her own journey, she has inspired countless women to embrace their strengths, overcome challenges, and make a lasting impact in their respective fields. Sandberg's unwavering determination, strategic mindset, and commitment to empowering women have positioned her as an iconic figure in the business world and a role model for aspiring female leaders.

You could also say the same for Mary Barra, the CEO of General Motors (GM). Barra made history as the first woman to lead a major global automaker. Under her leadership, GM underwent a significant transformation, focusing on innovation, electric and autonomous vehicles, and sustainability. Barra's inclusive leadership style and commitment to creating a diverse and inclusive workplace have driven positive change within the company. She has strongly advocated empowering women in the automotive industry and has implemented initiatives to promote gender equality and career advancement. Barra's resilience, strategic acumen, and ability to navigate challenges have positioned GM as a leader in the rapidly evolving automotive landscape. Her success story inspires women aspiring to break barriers and excel in traditionally male-dominated industries.

Like these women, I, too, have a story to tell. I spent the last 20 years of my career trying to hone in on my unique leadership style, and while I am still learning and growing, I am proud to say that I have helped dozens of females during my tenure. Many have advanced into leadership positions or even started their own businesses. If I can be a fearless leader, you can too!

Hear this now as you've never heard it before.

As a woman of incredible strength and potential, you harbor the power to shape your destiny and the course of this world. With every turn of the page in this tome of leadership, remember your influence; your reviews on Amazon can inspire countless others to take their leadership aspirations to heart.

Should you believe I have missed anything or have personal insights to share, please feel free to contribute your feedback. I am, like everyone, a constant work in progress, forever learning and evolving. I may not possess all the answers, but together, we can ignite a significant shift in empowering women of this generation.

May your journey be filled with joy, success, and all the rich experiences your resilient heart seeks and merits. With this newfound wisdom, embrace your leadership role, knowing you are paving the way for future women leaders.

To pay it forward and let other female leaders know about this book, click here or scan the QR code below to leave a review on Amazon.

Sign up for my newsletter here or scan the QR Code to hear more leadership strategies and learn about future projects & new book launches!

AUTHOR BIO

 Marguerite Allolding, born in a quaint New England town, is a trailblazing leader with over 20 years of experience in the professional world. At 43, she is now happily settled in New Jersey, living with her supportive husband and two beautiful children. Her journey took her from her small-town beginnings through the bustling corporate world of Chicago and finally to the metropolis of New York. Throughout this journey, she has held several esteemed leadership roles in large and small organizations, consistently breaking through glass ceilings.

During these years, Marguerite witnessed firsthand the untapped potential of countless talented women who were often overlooked or underestimated. This sparked a deep passion within her for empowering women and championing their voices, and inspired her to write *Fearless Female Leadership*.

Marguerite explores the multifaceted dimensions of female leadership in this meticulously researched and engagingly written book. She masterfully intertwines thought-provoking insights and compelling narratives, shedding light on women's unique strengths and struggles in positions of power. Marguerite is dedicated to paving the way for a future where female leadership is valued and recognized as a driving force of progress and innovation.

Her unwavering commitment to empowering women inspires everyone to strive for a more equitable and inclusive world. Marguerite Allolding stands as more than a leader; she is a shining beacon of hope and an embodiment of the strength inherent in fearless female leadership.

REFERENCES

AllBusiness. (2021, August 24). 3 Ways To Be More Authentic (And Successful) In Your Business. *Forbes*. https://www.forbes.com/sites/allbusiness/2021/08/24/3-ways-to-be-more-authentic-and-successful-in-your-business/?sh=24c4db7f5e67

Amplifying Women's Voices for Change. (n.d.). World Pulse. https://www.worldpulse.org/?gclid=CjwKCAjwl6OiBhA2EiwAuUwWZWTGQ3LnED8iecmViuMtixgGJXoL8utmIcBNYOaTGGejGmWoolo2DRoCtgEQAvD_BwE

Arscott, C. H. (2022, November 4). *A Better Approach to Networking*. Harvard Business Review. https://hbr.org/2022/11/a-better-approach-to-networking

A quote from The Open Door. (n.d.). https://www.goodreads.com/quotes/9605-life-is-either-a-daring-adventure-or-nothing-at-all

Authenticity Quotes (1309 quotes). (n.d.). https://www.goodreads.com/quotes/tag/authenticity#:~:text=%E2%80%9CWe%20have%20to%20dare%20to%20be%20ourselves%2C%20however%20frightening%20or%20strange%20that%20self%20may%20prove%20to%20be.%E2%80%9D%0A%E2%80%95%20May%20Sarton

Authenticity at Work: Everything You Need to Know. (n.d.). https://www.betterup.com/blog/authenticityatwork#:~:text=How%20to%20be,help%20you%20understand

Authentic Leadership: What It Is & Why It's Important | HBS Online. (2019, December 10). Business Insights Blog. https://online.hbs.edu/blog/post/authentic-leadership

Author. (2022, November 2). *The Maslow's Hierarchy of Needs for Employee Motivation*. Author, T., & Author, T. (2023). 5 Tips to Apply Maslow's Hierarchy of Needs in the Workplace. *Techfunnel*. https://www.techfunnel.com/hr-tech/maslows-hierarchy-workplace/

AttendanceBot Blog. https://www.attendancebot.com/blog/maslows-hierarchy-of-needs/#How_to_Apply_Maslows_Hierarchy_of_Needs_in_the_Workplace

Behind every woman is a Circle of women. Make it official. (n.d.). Lean In. https://leanin.org/circles?gclid=CjwKCAjwl6OiBhA2EiwAuUwWZS2ZWvHHTI71gvA6jC_QUKKgusLCDhTkOgvlp-Eu87L7FWi4KxsAehoCx-oQAvD_BwE

Bell, J. (2018, August 14). Listening Is An Underrated Leadership Tool. *Forbes*. https://www.forbes.com/sites/forbesdallascouncil/2018/08/14/listening-is-an-underrated-leadership-tool/?sh=4cb94b042fe5

Bhoumick, P. (2018). It's Really Matter: Review of the book, Emotional Intelligence: Why it can matter more than IQ' by Daniel Goleman. *Research Journal of Humanities and Social Sciences*. https://doi.org/10.5958/2321-5828.2018.00107.9

Biography: Indra Nooyi. (n.d.). National Women's History Museum. https://www.womenshistory.org/education-resources/biographies/indra-nooyi

Bishop, K. (2022, June 7). Why women have to sprint into leadership positions. *BBC Worklife*. https://www.bbc.com/worklife/article/20220603-why-women-have-to-sprint-into-leadership-positions

Blakely-Gray, R. (2021). Authenticity in Business: 7 Strategies to Become the Real McCoy. *Patriot Software for Small Business* https://smallbusiness.patriotsoftware.com/authenticity-in-business/#:-:text=On%20a%20scale,you%20get%20it%3F

Brim, B. B. J., EdD. (2023, March 30). How a Focus on People's Strengths Increases Their Work Engagement. *Gallup.com*. https://www.gallup.com/workplace/242096/focus-people-strengths-increases-work-engagement.aspx

Boss, J. (2014, June 12). 6 Principles Of A Leadership Legacy. *Forbes*. https://www.forbes.com/sites/jeffboss/2014/06/12/6-principles-of-a-leadership-legacy/?sh=5f0bc2044a51

Brush, K. (2020). upskilling. *WhatIs.com*. https://www.techtarget.com/whatis/definition/upskilling?Offer=abt_pubpro_AI-Insider

Boskamp, E. (2023). 35+ Compelling Workplace Collaboration Statistics [2023]: The Importance Of Teamwork. *Zippia*. https://www.zippia.com/advice/workplace-collaboration-statistics/

Change, I. (2020). What Is Growth Mindset and How to Achieve It. *Intelligent Change*. https://www.intelligentchange.com/blogs/read/what-is-growth-mindset-and-how-to-achieve-it

Cohn, A. (2021, October 11). *Don't Let Self-Doubt Hold You Back*. Harvard Business Review. https://hbr.org/2021/02/dont-let-self-doubt-hold-you-back

Conley, M. (2022, March 28). 45 Quotes That Celebrate Teamwork, Hard Work, and Collaboration. https://blog.hubspot.com/marketing/teamwork-quotes#:-:text=Quotes%20About%20Collaboration-,%22Alone%20we%20can%20do%20so%20little%3B%20together%20we%20can%20do%20so%20much.%22%20%E2%80%93%20Helen%20Keller,-%22Talent%20wins%20games

Denker, R. (2017, October 31). *5 Ways To Vastly Improve Your Strategic Visioning and Leadership.* https://www.rdpusa.com/5-ways-vastly-improve-strategic-visioning-leadership/

Dweck, C. (2023, April 6). *What Having a "Growth Mindset" Actually Means.* Harvard Business Review. https://hbr.org/2016/01/what-having-a-growth-mindset-actually-means

Elder, A. H. A. S. (2017, July 14). Why You Should Become a Published Writer as a Solopreneur. *Entrepreneur.* https://www.entrepreneur.com/article/295734

Elliott, E. (2021, December 23). 10 Ways to Be an Authentic Entrepreneur and Sell Your Best Self. *Entrepreneur.* https://www.entrepreneur.com/leadership/10-ways-to-be-an-authentic-entrepreneur-and-sell-your-best/403625#:~:text=In%20short%2C%20customers,a%20lot%20earlier.%22

Emotional Intelligence in Leadership: Why It's Important. (2019, April 3). Business Insights Blog. https://online.hbs.edu/blog/post/emotional-intelligence-in-leadership

Fallon, N. (2023). 35 Inspiring Leadership Quotes. *Business News Daily.* https://www.businessnewsdaily.com/7481-leadership-quotes.html

Fateh, A., Mustamil, N., & Shahzad, F. (2021). Role of authentic leadership and personal mastery in predicting employee creative behavior: A self-determination perspective. *Frontiers of Business Research in China, 15*(1), 1-16. https://doi.org/10.1186/s11782-021-00100-1

Find your leadership purpose and write a leadership purpose statement. (n.d.). Truist Leadership Institute. https://www.truistleadershipinstitute.com/publications-research/media-publications/find-your-leadership-purpose-and-write-a-leadership-purpose-statement

FutureLearn. (2023, April 14). *How to improve leadership skills: 7 top tips – FutureLearn.* https://www.futurelearn.com/info/blog/how-to-improve-leadership-skills#1_Identify_your_strengths_and_weaknesses

Future Talent Learning. (n.d.). *What are the top 5 characteristics of emotional intelligence in good leadership?* https://www.futuretalentlearning.com/en/future-talent-learning-blog/what-are-the-top-5-characteristics-of-emotional-intelligence-in-good-leadership

Georgeac, O. a. M. (2021). Are Leaders Rewarded for Taking Risks? *Yale Insights.* https://insights.som.yale.edu/insights/are-leaders-rewarded-for-taking-risks

Goleman, D., Boyatzis, R. E., & McKee, A. (2013). *Primal Leadership: Unleashing the Power of Emotional Intelligence.* Harvard Business Press.

Goleman, D. (2023, April 4). *What Makes a Leader?* Harvard Business Review. https://hbr.org/2004/01/what-makes-a-leader

Goodman, N. (2013, March 14). Train Your Brain to Overcome Fear. *Entrepreneur*. https://www.entrepreneur.com/starting-a-business/train-your-brain-to-overcome-fear/226050

Green, H. (2023, March 29). *Active Listening As A Leadership Skill | Vistage*. Vistage Research Center. https://www.vistage.com/research-center/business-leadership/20180912-active-listening-leadership-skill/

Greenwood, S. (2023, March 1). *The gender wage gap endures in the U.S. | Pew Research Center*. Pew Research Center's Social & Demographic Trends Project. https://www.pewresearch.org/social-trends/2023/03/01/the-enduring-grip-of-the-gender-pay-gap/

Hannah. (2020, February 25). *Top 10 Quotes for Growth Mindset | SATs Companion*. SATs Companion. https://satscompanion.com/top-10-quotes-growth-mindset/

Harper, T. (2021, March 2). Blogging Tips & Events for Content Creators Everywhere | Blogher. *Blogging Tips &Amp; Events for Content Creators Everywhere | Blogher*. https://www.blogher.com/feature/leadership-skills-of-successful-women-687/

Hickey, K. F. (2016, November 23). *5 lessons from Skillshare: on empowering team members to do their best work*. Wavelength by Asana. https://wavelength.asana.com/workstyle-skillshare/

Herrity, J. (2022). Maslow's Hierarchy of Needs: Applying It in the Workplace. *Indeed.com*. https://www.indeed.com/career-advice/career-development/maslows-hierarchy-of-needs

Home - Grace Hopper Celebration. (2023, July 3). Grace Hopper Celebration. https://ghc.anitab.org/

Hopper, E. (2020). Maslow's Hierarchy of Needs Explained. *ThoughtCo*. https://www.thoughtco.com/maslows-hierarchy-of-needs-4582571

Houseofself. (2021). 5 Ways to Reframe Your Fear of Failure. *House of Self*. https://houseofself.co.uk/5-ways-to-reframe-your-fear-of-failure/

Ibarra, H. (2019, August 22). *Women and the Vision Thing*. Harvard Business Review. https://hbr.org/2009/01/women-and-the-vision-thing

Ibarra, H. (2019, February 7). *How Leaders Create and Use Networks*. Harvard Business Review. https://hbr.org/2007/01/how-leaders-create-and-use-networks

Indeed Editorial Team. (2023). How To Find Purpose in Your Work (Benefits, Steps and Tips). *Indeed.com*. https://www.indeed.com/career-advice/career-development/purpose-in-work

Indeed Editorial Team. (2023). How To Leverage Your Strengths in the Workplace. *Indeed.com*. https://www.indeed.com/career-advice/career-development/leveraging-strengths

Indeed Editorial Team. (2023). 10 Benefits of Effective Communication in the Workplace. *Indeed.com*. https://www.indeed.com/career-advice/career-development/communication-benefits

Indeed Editorial Team. (2022). What Is Innovative Leadership? *Indeed.com*. https://www.indeed.com/career-advice/career-development/innovative-leadership

Indeed Editorial Team. (2022). 56 Inspiring Team Communication Quotes To Motivate Your Team. *Indeed.com*. https://www.indeed.com/career-advice/career-development/team-communication-quotes

James, G. (2021, January 5). Science Says: Women in Business Outperform Men. *Inc.com*: https://www.inc.com/geoffrey-james/science-says-woman-in-business-outperform-men.html

Journeytoleadershipblog. (2019). The Importance Of Risk Taking In Leadership. *Journey to Leadership*. https://journeytoleadershipblog.com/2019/04/01/risk-taking-in-leadership/

Karen Salmansohn Quotes (Author of How to Be Happy, Dammit). (n.d.). https://www.goodreads.com/author/quotes/117096.Karen_Salmansohn

Larson, K. (2023, March 8). 31 Big Questions About Business Coaching & Executive Coaching Answered. *Champion PSI*. https://www.championpsi.com/blog/31-big-questions-about-business-coaching-executive-coaching-answered/

Leadership Courses: Online Training to Inspire and Lead. (n.d.). Udemy. https://www.udemy.com/courses/personal-development/leadership/?search-query=leadership&utm_source=adwords&utm_medium=udemyads&utm_campaign=DSA_Catchall_la.EN_cc.ROW&utm_content=deal4584&utm_term=_._ag_88010211481_._ad_535397282064_._kw__._de_c_._dm__._pl__._ti_dsa-391663266418_._li_9053242_._pd__._&matchtype=&gclid=CjwKCAjw9J2iBhBPEiwAErwpecu9x3qyuhLjWK9TvXOS8IleMtouQQbPsCofoqicZKOUA503DJXqNhoC500QAvD_BwE

Legacy Quotes. (n.d.). BrainyQuote. https://www.brainyquote.com/topics/legacy-quotes

Leverage Your Leadership Skills To Improve Your Impact | How To Be A Leader | Leadership And Management | Leadership Skills | Leadership Development | International Institute of Directors and Managers | IIDM - IIDM Global. (n.d.). https://www.iidmglobal.com/expert_talk/expert-talk-categories/leadership/leadership_skill/id38810.html

Llego, M. A. (2022). The Benefits of Achieving Self-Actualization. *TeacherPH*. https://www.teacherph.com/achieving-self-actualization/

Kitchens, J. (2022, September 6). How to Be an Adaptable Leader and Use Change to Your Advantage. *Entrepreneur*. https://www.entrepreneur.com/leadership/how-to-be-an-adaptable-leader-and-use-change-to-your/428557

LinkedIn. (n.d.). https://www.linkedin.com/pulse/do-you-have-fixed-growth-mindset-linda-scott/

LinkedIn. (n.d.). https://www.linkedin.com/pulse/impact-company-culture-employee-retention-business-umbrella/

LinkedIn. (n.d.). https://www.linkedin.com/pulse/maslows-hierarchy-needs-benefits-self-actualized-employees-scott-king/

LinkedIn. (n.d.). https://www.linkedin.com/pulse/5-reasons-why-people-avoid-taking-risks-munyaradzi-demadema/

LinkedIn. (n.d.). https://www.linkedin.com/pulse/3-proven-ways-more-persistent-leadership-john-eades/

Lonczak, H. S., PhD. (2023). 40 Emotional Intelligence Quotes & Do They Ring True? *PositivePsychology.com*. https://positivepsychology.com/emotional-intelligence-quotes/

Maldonado, Y. (2022, June 6). Over 30% of Americans Suffer From Impostor Syndrome, Study Finds. *NBC10 Philadelphia*. https://www.nbcphiladelphia.com/news/local/over-30-of-americans-suffer-from-impostor-syndrome-study-finds/3259530/

Mark Zuckerberg Quotes. (n.d.). BrainyQuote. https://www.brainyquote.com/quotes/mark_zuckerberg_453450

McCarthy, D. (2022, December 1). *12 Ways to Become a More Confident Leader – Pragmatic Institute Resources*. Pragmatic Institute Resources. https://www.pragmaticinstitute.com/resources/articles/product/12-ways-to-develop-leadership-confidence/

Mcleod, S., PhD. (2023). Maslow's Hierarchy of Needs. *Simply Psychology*. https://www.simplypsychology.org/maslow.html

Mentoring activities: 17 examples to try in your next meeting | Together Mentoring Software. (n.d.). https://www.togetherplatform.com/blog/mentoring-activities-to-try

MindTools | Home. (n.d.). https://www.mindtools.com/aal02x7/essential-negotiation-skills

Morgan, J. (2021, December 16). Why Great Leaders Are Risk-Takers - Jacob Morgan - Medium. *Medium*. https://medium.com/jacob-morgan/why-great-leaders-are-risk-takers-22e031313391

Morgan, O. (2021). How to Define Your Purpose as a Leader — Morgan Latif. *Morgan Latif*. https://morganlatif.com/resources/how-to-define-your-purpose-as-a-leader

Morin, A. (2023). Growth Mindset: How to Develop Growth Mindset. *Understood*. https://www.understood.org/en/articles/growth-mindset

MSEd, K. C. (2022). Maslow's Hierarchy of Needs. *Verywell Mind*. https://www.verywellmind.com/what-is-maslows-hierarchy-of-needs-4136760

Nemeth, A. (2020, April 16). 20 Quotes to Inspire You to Find More Purpose in Your Work. *MovingWorlds Blog*. https://blog.movingworlds.org/purpose-at-work-quotes/

Ntsoane, M. (2023, July 15). Helpful tips to discover your PURPOSE as a leader - Esme Witbooi Coaching. *Esme Witbooi Coaching*. https://www.esmelifecoaching.com/helpful-tips-to-discover-your-purpose-as-leader/

Patel, N. (2020). Truth Will Out – Why Authenticity is the Key to Growing Your Business. *Neil Patel*. https://neilpatel.com/blog/truth-will-out/

Patterson, A. R. (2023, July 6). *Richard Patterson*. NetLdn. https://netldn.uk/author/richardpattersonnz/

Pew Research Center Finds Gender Pay Gap Has Barely Budged in Past 20 Years. (2023). *Lexology*. https://www.lexology.com/library/detail.aspx?g=8ad4ecf7-7bff-4ffe-afcf-3cf1f05482d8

Pierce, M. (2022, July 28). *How to Leverage Your Leadership Style for Business Success - Addicted 2 Success*. Addicted 2 Success. https://addicted2success.com/success-advice/how-to-leverage-your-leadership-style-for-business-success/

Risks Quotes. (n.d.). BrainyQuote. https://www.brainyquote.com/topics/risks-quotes

Robbins, M., & Robbins, M. (2022). The Trap of Comparison with Others. *Mike Robbins | Infusing Life and Business With Authenticity and Appreciation*. https://mike-robbins.com/the-trap-of-comparison/

Ruderman, M. (2022). How to Increase Your Resilience as a Leader. *CCL*. https://www.ccl.org/articles/leading-effectively-articles/4-tips-will-increase-resiliency-leader/

Runyon, M. (n.d.). *How active listening can make you a better leader*. The Enterprisers Project. https://enterprisersproject.com/article/2021/11/how-active-listening-can-make-you-better-leader

Ruth Bader Ginsburg Tells Young Women: "Fight For The Things You Care About" | Radcliffe Institute for Advanced Study at Harvard University. (n.d.). Radcliffe Institute for Advanced Study at Harvard University. https://www.radcliffe.harvard.edu/news-and-ideas/ruth-bader-ginsburg-tells-young-women-fight-for-the-things-you-care-about

Schinkel, M. (2023, July 20). 9 Tips for Leading with Integrity - ACHIEVE Centre for Leadership. *ACHIEVE Centre for Leadership*. https://achievecentre.com/blog/9-tips-for-leading-with-integrity/

Scott, L. (n.d.). Do you have a fixed or a growth mindset? *www.linkedin.com*. https://www.linkedin.com/pulse/do-you-have-fixed-growth-mindset-linda-scott/?trk=articles_directory

Sharon. (2023). Great Leaders Take Risks. *SIGMA Assessment Systems*. https://www.sigmaassessmentsystems.com/great-leaders-risk-taking/

Simkins, M. D. (2021, January 5). How Successful Leaders Overcome Self-Doubt. *Inc.com*. https://www.inc.com/melissa-dawn-simkins/4-ways-to-crush-self-doubt-when-your-inner-critic-gets-best-of-you.html

Slack. (n.d.). *Collaborative leadership: an inclusive way to manage virtual teams*. Slack. https://slack.com/blog/collaboration/collaborative-leadership-top-down-team-centric

Staff, L. E. (2023). The Top 6 Rules of Leadership Networking. *CCL*. https://www.ccl.org/articles/leading-effectively-articles/top-6-rules-leadership-networking/

Staff, L. E. (2023). 15 Tips for Effective Communication in Leadership. *CCL*. https://www.ccl.org/articles/leading-effectively-articles/communication-1-idea-3-facts-5-tips/

Staff, L. E. (2022). 8 Steps to More Resilient Leadership. *CCL*. https://www.ccl.org/articles/leading-effectively-articles/8-steps-help-become-resilient/

Strategic thinking skills | Robert Half. (2021, September 6). https://www.roberthalf.co.nz/career-advice/career-development/strategic-thinking-skills

Susancfoster. (2020). 7 Leadership Skills of Successful Women. *LH AGENDA*. https://lhagenda.com/career/7-leadership-skills-of-successful-women/

Tech, F. (2020). null. *Florida Tech Online*. https://www.floridatechonline.com/blog/business/problem-solving-a-critical-leadership-skill/

Technavio. (2020, May 11). Global Corporate Leadership Training Market 2020-2024 | Increased Spending on Corporate Leadership Training to Boost Market Growth | Technavio. *Business Wire.* https://www.businesswire.com/news/home/20200311005401/en/Global-Corporate-Leadership-Training-Market-2020-2024-Increased-Spending-on-Corporate-Leadership-Training-to-Boost-Market-Growth-Technavio

Thakrar, M. (2020, January 16). How To Become An Adaptable Leader. *Forbes.* https://www.forbes.com/sites/forbescoachescouncil/2020/01/16/how-to-become-an-adaptable-leader/?sh=74f3c11c14b6

Tina. (2023). Leadership Statistics: Demographics and Development in 2023. *TeamStage.* https://teamstage.io/leadership-statistics/

Tonya.Johnson. (2023). 12 tips for overcoming imposter syndrome in leadership. *Fast Company.* https://www.fastcompany.com/90862289/12-tips-for-overcoming-imposter-syndrome-in-leadership

Top 10 Skills for Aspiring Female Leaders | The International Educator (TIE Online). (n.d.). https://www.tieonline.com/article/3247/top-10-skills-for-aspiring-female-leaders

Top 25 Quotes by Maya Angelou (of 1010) | A-Z Quotes. (n.d.). A-Z Quotes. https://www.azquotes.com/author/440-Maya_Angelou

Trust in the Workplace: 10 Steps to Build Trust with Employees. (n.d.). https://www.yourthoughtpartner.com/blog/bid/59619/leaders-follow-these-6-steps-to-build-trust-with-employees-improve-how-you-re-perceived

Uță, I. (2023, June 16). 12 Leadership Styles for Successful Leaders (complete list) with Pros & Cons - BRAND MINDS. *BRAND MINDS.* https://brandminds.com/12-leadership-styles-for-successful-leaders-complete-list-with-pros-cons

Valamis. (2023, April 19). Leadership Communication. *Valamis.* https://www.valamis.com/hub/leadership-communication

Valamis. (2023, March 20). Emotional Intelligence in the Workplace. *Valamis.* https://www.valamis.com/hub/emotional-intelligence-in-the-workplace

Wallbridge, A., & Wallbridge, A. (2023). The Importance Of Self-Awareness In Emotional Intelligence. *TSW Training.* https://www.tsw.co.uk/blog/leadership-and-management/self-awareness-in-emotional-intelligence/#:~:text=Self%2Dawareness%20is%20the%20ability,of%20other%20%E2%80%9Csoft%20skills%E2%80%9D

Weller, C., Hickey, W., Kiersz, A., & Su, J. L. (2021, May 29). Most Americans are burned out from the pandemic. These charts reveal the biggest stressors we're facing right now. *Busi-*

ness Insider. https://www.businessinsider.com/american-burnout-survey-results-age-race-job-region-covid-2021-5#:~:text=There%27s%20a%20stark%20gender%20gap%20in%20self-reported%20burnout.,out%2C%20compared%20to%20only%2055%25%20of%20male%20respondents.

What Authentic Leadership Is and Why Showing Up As Yourself Matters. (n.d.). https://www.betterup.com/blog/authentic-leadership

Why Authenticity in DEI Practices in the Workplace Leads to Good Business. (n.d.). https://partnerstack.com/articles/dei-practices-authenticity-workplace-matters

Why diversity matters. (2015, January 1). McKinsey & Company. https://www.mckinsey.com/capabilities/people-and-organizational-performance/our-insights/why-diversity-matters

Why consistency is important in leadership. (n.d.). https://www.morningcoach.com/blog/why-consistency-is-important-in-leadership

Women in Leadership - How to Promote? (n.d.). Tutorialspoint. https://www.tutorialspoint.com/women_in_leadership/women_in_leadership_how_to_promote.htm

WomensMedia. (2021, February 1). Leadership When You Have Imposter Syndrome. *Forbes.* https://www.forbes.com/sites/womensmedia/2021/02/01/leadership-when-you-have-imposter-syndrome/?sh=5c7076387195

Zenger, J. (2021, March 24). The Extremely Curious Case Of Women's Strategic Thinking. *Forbes*: https://www.forbes.com/sites/jackzenger/2021/03/24/the-extremely-curious-case-of-womens-strategic-thinking/?sh=53dea236c1c6

Ziegler, P. (2022, December 22). How To Become An Inspirational Female Leader In 2023? *Best Diplomats | Diplomatic Conferences | New York.* https://bestdiplomats.org/how-to-become-inspirational-female-leaders/

4 Ways to Conquer Your Fears and Take Smarter Risks | BusinessCollective. (2013, November 14). BusinessCollective. https://businesscollective.com/4-ways-to-conquer-your-fears-and-take-smarter-risks/index.html

5 Benefits of Effective Leadership Communication. (n.d.). SMU Academy. https://academy.smu.edu.sg/insights/5-benefits-effective-leadership-communication-7826

7 steps to leaving a lasting legacy | Tony Robbins. (2023, June 2). tonyrobbins.com. https://www.tonyrobbins.com/business/how-to-leave-a-legacy/

8 Essential Leadership Communication Skills | HBS Online. (2019, November 14). Business Insights Blog. https://online.hbs.edu/blog/post/leadership-communication

8 Leadership Qualities to Motivate Your Team | DeakinCo. (2023, May 3). DeakinCo. | Powering Workplace Performance. https://deakinco.com/resource/8-leadership-qualities-to-motivate-and-inspire-your-team/

Also by Marguerite Allolding

9 POWERFUL STRATEGIES THAT ENCOURAGE DIVERSITY,
FOSTER EQUITY, AND CULTIVATE
INCLUSIVITY TO TRANSFORM YOUR WORKPLACE

IMPACTFUL
INCLUSIVE
LEADERSHIP

MARGUERITE ALLOLDING

Click link or scan QR code below to find IMPACTFUL INCLUSIVE LEADERSHIP: 9 Powerful Strategies That Encourage Diversity, Foster Equity, and Cultivate Inclusivity to Transform Your Workplace.

Also by Marguerite Allolding

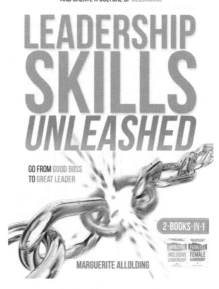

Click link or scan QR code below to find Leadership Skills Unleashed: 18 Transformative Strategies for Managers at Any Level – Develop a Growth Mindset, Overcome Imposter Syndrome, and Create a Culture of Belonging

Made in United States
Cleveland, OH
29 October 2024

10356739R00077